Kaare Grønbæ

An Introduction to C

MW01088046

Kaare Grønbech / John R. Krueger

An Introduction to Classical (Literary) Mongolian

Introduction, Grammar, Reader, Glossary

Third corrected edition

1993

Harrassowitz Verlag · Wiesbaden

Bibliografische Information der Deutschen Nationalbibliothek
Die Deutsche Nationalbibliothek verzeichnet diese Publikation in der Deutschen
Nationalbibliografie; detaillierte bibliografische Daten sind im Internet
über https://dnb.de abrufbar.

Bibliographic information published by the Deutsche Nationalbibliothek
The Deutsche Nationalbibliothek lists this publication in the Deutsche Nationalbibliografie;
detailed bibliographic data are available in the internet
at https://dnb.de.

For further information about our publishing program consult our
website http://www.harrassowitz-verlag.de
© Otto Harrassowitz GmbH & Co. KG, Wiesbaden 1993
Printed on permanent/durable paper.
Printing and binding: KN Digital Printforce GmbH, Stuttgart
Printed in Germany

ISBN 978-3-447-03298-8

Table of Contents

Preface to the Third Edition

The continued sale of this small grammar makes it possible for the publishers to offer a third printing, and I have taken advantage of this to re-organize the additions made in the Second Edition into the main body of the text. There still remain many precious points which can be expanded and which thoughtful correspondents and users have brought to light over the decades. To engage on a complete re-writing would overstep the planned bounds of this Introduction; fuller information is the province of such a book as N. Poppe's *Grammar of Written Mongolian* (Wiesbaden, O. Harrassowitz, 4th unrev. edition, 1991), which gives a more advanced treatment. The instructor will be able to expand on these issues and give additional commentary.

The present work proposes to afford a brief and practical introduction to classical and literary Mongolian, paying special heed to the requirements of those who may pursue their study otherwise unaided. The plan of the work is as follows. The progressive exposition of the grammatical structure is paralleled by Mongolian reading selections, which incorporate the new features illustrated in the lesson. Since the grammar is drawn from the reading material, exceptions, minor variations and little-used forms are dealt with not at all, or only slightly. Since this is not a work for the specialist, references to parallel features in Turkic and other languages, as well as comments on the origin and development of forms, have been kept to a minimum or omitted altogether. Use of the Mongolian script is deferred until the student is prepared with a knowledge of the grammar and has a stock of basic words at his command.

There is a brief introduction of very general character, which gives broad outlines of Mongolian history, life, institutions and customs, and some political, economic and social data on Mongolia past and present. When this was written in 1955, and even when it was updated in 1975, there was a great lack of such general information on Mongolian in English. Now of course, almost another 20 years later, there is an abundance of sources in English and European languages, and many readers will already be aware that Mongolia has long been a member of the United Nations, that the U.S. and Mongolia finally established diplomatic relations in 1989, and perhaps even of the latest development, the re-introduction of the historic vertical Mongolian (Uighur) script. This should be borne in mind when reading that introductory portion today. The two former editions likewise contained some sections which have been eliminated as now no longer needed: these were a chronology, a bibliography now outmoded, a sketch of modern Khalkha, and so on.

The death of the senior author, Professor K. Grønbech, in 1957, made impossible any revision of this book which could represent the views of both authors. Still the reactions of readers and reviewers, and especially the experience of teaching students from the book over quite a few years, produced a body of corrections and clarifications which have been integrated into the present edition. As I shared with my teacher an uncomfortable feeling about the phrase "Written Mongolian" (German *Schriftmongolisch*), we devised the term "Classical (Literary) Mongolian" for our title, and meant it to cover both the strictly classical language of the great Buddhist translations (mid-17th through 18th century) as well as the later similar literary language in vertical script. To say "literary Mongolian" might be a better solution today, and to set certain boundaries of date and form usage to define the term, but I retain the old title for continuity.

The small reader which accompanied Professor Grønbech's university lectures on Mongolian was his privately circulated *Mongolske tekster i originalskrift* (Copenhagen, 1945), intended for development into an anthology of Mongolian literature. To fill the need for old-script reading material to accompany this grammar, I later independently prepared for my classes, from the original sources, a new edition of most of the materials earlier selected by him, together with my own notes and additions. It appeared as *Supplementary Texts in Mongolian Script For first Year Readings,** and can serve as logical companion to this grammar. Moreover, the glossary of this grammar is already fully keyed to the vocabulary required there, so that no other dictionary is needed.

Since I have, I confess, so often during the years referred to this as „my" grammar, permit me here to make a few remarks on the cooperation between the senior author and myself. During my second term as a foreign student at Copenhagen (early 1953), I attended Grønbech's lectures on Classical Mongolian, which he presented in formal fashion and accompanied with some brief reading passages chosen by him. During that summer, it occurred to me to arrange the readings in a graded order and on that basis, create an expository practical grammar in which the illustrative reading nicely parallels the grammar just presented. It was so to speak written backwards from the readings, which has made it quite effective in teaching. Without Grønbech having prepared his scheme of presentation, I would not have learned the elements; and without my having reorganized his scheme into a new fashion, his information would have gone little further. Hence, it proved a fine and equal cooperation for each of us with good results. I did not have at that time the depth of knowledge from reading to enable any independent creation, and further the time was then quite suitable to present such a work to the public. I still cherish his evaluation of my draft, when first presented to him in the fall of 1953, to the effect of, „Exactly the way I would have prepared it myself." It was a great loss that he lived only a couple of years beyond that time. I owe that kindly and learned man so much.

September 7, 1992   John R. Krueger

---

* It may be obtained from The Mongolia Society, Goodbody Hall 321-322, Indiana University, Bloomington, Indiana 47405 USA; Special Papers Issue Four, 1965, 43 pp. The price is now US $ 7.50 plus mailing.

Acknowledgments

Mr. Krueger's studies in Denmark (1952—1954) were made possible by grants from the United States Educational Foundation in Denmark, which administers funds available under the Fulbright Act.
For much assistance, valuable suggestions and corrections and untiring interest our thanks are due to Professor N. Poppe, Seattle, and Mr. K. Thomsen, M. A., Copenhagen. The authors, however, assume full responsibility for their own errors of fact or judgment.

I. Introduction

Historical Background

At the beginning of the 13th century, mediæval Europe was relatively complacent except for the shifting fortunes of the Crusaders, who in 1204 had taken and sacked Constantinople. Political and religious controversy such as the sporadic armed conflict between the Moslem and Christian spheres and the internal dissensions between the Roman Catholic and Eastern Orthodox branches of the Christian church served both to weaken Europe within and to distract attention from events in the world without.

Then, with little or no warning, catastrophe fell.

Arising from the barren plateau of Mongolia, fierce armies of nomadic horsemen swept across the broad plains and steppes of Central Asia, sacking and laying cities waste, putting whole populations to the sword and in general crushing civilizations and destroying cultures in their path. In the brief span of 30 years (1211—1241), the roving Mongol hordes of Genghis Khan and his successors overran most of Europe and Asia, and made themselves masters of a vast empire which ranged from the Yellow Sea in the Far East and drove a wedge into the heart of Central Eastern Europe, the Hungarian *alföld* (lower plain). Europe trembled before the dreadful calamity doubtless about to be imposed by these all-engulfing conquerors who devastated everyone who dared oppose them. Had the Mongol barbarian ravages gone unchecked, the dissolute governments would surely have toppled before the onslaught of these warlike invaders already battering at the gates. This would have spelled the doom of Western civilization, and it is doubtful if it would have recovered for many centuries.

As it was, though, on the eve of certain victory, the Mongol tribesmen turned back from the threshold of Europe as mysteriously and quickly as they had come. Internal affairs of state arising from the death of Genghis Khan's son and successor, Ögedei, recalled the Mongol princes to Mongolia to vie with each other in being elected the new Khan. In any event, they were more interested in the riches of China or even in uniting the Turco-Mongol peoples than enslaving all of Europe, but no Mongol leader after Ögedei could muster sufficient strength and unity among the loosely knit clans to return to Europe. Because they withdrew of their own accord, European statesmen were never quite certain for centuries when a new scourge from the East would descend on them to cleanse and chastise their decadent monarchies.

The moment of Mongol glory had come and gone. But in spite of carnage and slaughter on a scale the world had never known, the Mongols freed the long overland trade route from China to the West, and paved the way for introduction of Eastern arts, crafts, inventions and discoveries, such as gunpowder and printing. But who were these Mongols? Where did they come from and why? How can it be that they almost conquered the then known world? The Mongols were certain tribes of Eastern Asia, whose leader Temüjin (1167?—1227) united his loosely bound nomad clansmen, supplemented by some Turco-Tatar peoples, into a supreme fighting force. He was crowned Emperor in 1206 and given the name *Chinggis* (variously transcribed, mainly through Persian sources, as Jingis, Genghis, *etc.*) and the title *Qagan* (transcribed as Khan, Khagan, *etc.*). It was not, as many once supposed, desiccation of tribal pasture lands that gave rise to the imperialistic eruption of the Mongols in the 13th century. The Mongol advance was merely the last great wave in a cycle of westward expansion of nomadic groups, much like their predecessors, the Huns, under Attila. Although the efficacy of their military methods cannot be disputed, the Mongol cycle was in the upward swing of strength, while that of the conquered peoples was in the downward swing of decline. Their remarkable success in warfare can be attributed not only to their superb organization, discipline and leadership, but also to their unbelievably hardy men and sturdy horses, who travelled great distances with a minimum of food and rest, and then overcame by skill numerically superior foes. At the height of their conquests, a nation of about a million subjugated other nations with a total population of over a hundred million. Without doubt, the Mongol invaders left their mark on European history.

The Mongolia of today

Mongolia is now purely a geographical location; linguistically and politically there are several Mongolias. In historical times, the nomads ranged far and wide across the steppes and deserts, but now with the formation of political boundaries not freely passable, the tribes are more or less established in specific areas.

The largest and most significant Mongol state is the Mongolian People's Republic (*bügüde nairamdaqu mongγol arad ulus*), which before 1924 was known as Outer Mongolia, because of its greater distance from Peking (Peiping), seat of the Manchu dynasty in China. It occupies an area of 606,000 sq. miles (as large as the United States east of the Mississippi river and north of the Ohio river), and is located somewhat northwest of China, south of Siberia and west of Manchuria. Its capital Ulān Bātur (*ulaγan baγatur*, red hero), which was formerly called Urga (*örgege*, residence of a prince), lies about 900 miles due northwest of Tientsin on the Yellow Sea, on a line which crosses Peking and Kalgan, the latter for centuries the traditional gateway to Mongolia (the name indeed derives from *qaγalγan*, gate).

Mountains are found along most of the north, northwest and southwest, while along the southern border of Outer Mongolia, lies the famous

Gobi (*γobi*, desert), a desolate plateau stretching some 600 miles south-west-northeast, about 3,000 feet above sea-level.
Published statistics on the population are at considerable variance with each other. There are somewhat under a million Mongols in the Mongolian People's Republic. The major dialect in the MPR is the Khalkha.
Inner Mongolia, which never had an independent political existence, has been absorbed into northwest China, namely the four provinces of Ninghsia, Suiyüan, Chahar and Jehol. It lies south and southeast of the MPR, forming a belt between it and the Great Wall of China. There are perhaps less than a million Mongols in Inner Mongolia, and they have lost much ground in recent years to the relentless advance of Chinese colonization, which overshadows them economically, and dominates them politically. The major dialects are the Chahar and Ordos.
Contiguous to the MPR, and directly north of Ulān Bātur, lies the Buryat Mongol ASSR, which is a part of the Soviet Union. The capital and chief city is Ulān Ude (*ulaγan egüde*, red gate), formerly Verkhneudinsk. About a quarter of a million Mongols speak Buryat dialects. The best known geographical feature is Lake Baikal, which divides the cisbaikalian (northwestern) from the transbaikalian (southeastern) section.
In addition to these major divisions, there is a considerable quantity of Mongols in the Hsingan province of Manchuria, much under a million, divided into a number of tribes whose dialects are mostly related to those of Inner Mongolia. Perhaps a million Mongols are scattered throughout the Chinese province of Sinkiang (Chinese Turkestan), to the southwest and west of the MPR, in the Koko-Noor (*köke nayur*, blue lake) district of northeastern Tibet, and until recently in the distant Kalmyk territory on the lower Volga near the Caspian Sea. In Central Afghanistan some tribesmen still retain their Mongol dialect.

The Mongols

Physically, the Mongols are short-statured, with yellowish skin and black hair: their features are with broad noses, prominent cheekbones, and slanting eyes, set in a generally flat face. They are organized into tribes and clans, and lay great stress on family ancestry and genealogy. They live mostly in round felt tents, which are quickly disassembled and suited to their way of life.
The traditional, and still major, occupation of the Mongols is livestock breeding, which provides the essential human needs of housing, clothing and food. The animals raised are camels, horses, cattle, sheep and goats. Hunting, especially of furbearing animals, is a profitable sideline for many Mongols, but farming, owing to the sandy, stony ground, is virtually impossible except in a few river valleys. Although the essentially nomadic life of most of the population, moving their herds

from pasture to pasture, is not conducive to industry or manufacturing, there is some mining of coal and sulphur, and some tannery and dairy industry.

In religion, the Mongols are Buddhists, this religion having been finally introduced in 1577 after several unsuccessful attempts on the part of various emperors and princes as far back as the 13th century. The spiritual head of their faith is the Dalai Lama of Tibet. Buddhism revolutionized the habits of the Mongols by gradually tying them to places where there were temples. This played an important part in converting them from a nation of nomadic warriors into placid herdsmen.

After the turn of the century, and before the establishment of the MPR, Mongolia and Central Asia in general were the scene of various scientific expeditions to collect geological, archeological and palaeontological data, with a view to confirming theories that Central Asian plateaus had been a cradle of development for dominant mammalian species. Rich fossil remains were discovered on the Kalgan-Urga road, and in the central desert of Mongolia were discovered the famous dinosaur eggs popularized by recent writers.

Recent Political Events in the MPR

When the Manchu dynasty finally collapsed in 1911, under pressure of continued uprisings by revolutionaries such as Sun Yat sen, China adopted a republican form of government. The Mongol princes took advantage of this to throw off the Chinese yoke and established the so-called Living Buddha (*qutuytu*) as ruler. The territory of Outer Mongolia see-sawed between Russia and China until the early twenties, when in 1921 a Soviet-inspired People's Republic was set up. A constitution patterned after that of the USSR was adopted in 1924, and the young Soviet protectorate gradually introduced measures which considerably changed the largely feudal society by abolishing theocratic rule (aided by the death of the Qutuqtu in 1924), reducing the numbers of lamas (which formerly claimed a third of the male population), establishing an army, and adding other features of a modern state.

The non-existence of foreign relations with nations other than the Soviet bloc, and the growing close collaboration between the MPR and the USSR have made it a political satellite of the Soviet Union. It was not until after the Second World War, however, when China itself had fallen to the Communist advance, that Mongolia was officially recognized as independent by the Chinese in 1946.

In the governmental structure of the MPR, representation of the people is carried out in a bicameral assembly, the Great *qural* and the Small *qural*. The Prime Minister or Premier, until his death in 1952, was Marshal Choibalsang. The incumbent is Tsedenbal.

Since 1924, few Westerners (except some Soviet citizens) have been permitted to enter the MPR, and our knowledge of events there is based almost entirely on second-hand sources. The American vice-president, Henry Wallace, did visit Ulān Bātur briefly in 1944 on his tour of the Soviet Union. The Western world was given another glimpse of Mongol fighting strength when in 1945, just before the Japanese surrender, a small but well-equipped Mongol army together with Soviet forces attacked Japanese installations in Manchuria and Inner Mongolia. After a brief and successful campaign, the Mongols retired. In 1946, the application of the MPR for membership in the United Nations was rejected, chiefly because it was felt that information about conditions in Mongolia was lacking, and that this reflected on the Mongols' ability to engage in international relations. In 1961, Mongolia was admitted to the UN, and in January 1989 diplomatic relations were established between the Mongolian and the United States.

The Mongolian Language

The Mongolian language usually ranks as a member of the Altaic family of languages, whose three major divisions are the Manchurian (or Tungus), the Mongolian, and the Turkic (or Turco-Tatar) groups of languages. The supposed genetic affiliation of these groups has never been proved, but the practical utilization of the term 'Altaic languages' lies in the presence of common traits in the syntax, general structure and vocabularies of the three language families.

Mongolian is characterized *inter alia* by vowel harmony, absence of initial and final consonant clusters, non-existence of long consonants, absence of gender and a general agglutination of suffixes. The subject generally occurs first in a sentence, and the verb in final position, with other modifying elements arranged between them. Syntactically, the sentences are periodic, being joined by various gerunds and participles, which correspond to the relative clauses and sequence of tenses of Western languages.

The tradition of the written language rests on a very old basis. Writing was introduced under Chinggis Qagan in the early 13th century, by borrowing the vertical script of the Uighurs (who had taken it from the Sogdians). Although the script is alphabetical, it can often be ambiguous, as many letters, especially *t / d*, *k / g*, *o / u*, and *ö / ü*, are not distinguished from each other.

Ancient Mongolian is the Mongolian language in the 12th and 13th centuries. When it was committed to writing in 1204 (if we accept the Mongol tradition), it already reflected a somewhat earlier pronunciation.

Classical Mongolian is the literary language as it was treated by the translators of the Tibetan lamaistic canon, the Kanjur, under the zealous Mongol emperor Legdan Qagan (1604—1634). It was fixed in its final form by the revised edition xylographed in Peking in 1720, and in this latter shape has remained the literary norm to the present day. The second part of the canon, the Tanjur, followed in 1749.

There has been no inner development of the literary language, except insofar as scribes in the last several centuries tend to avoid words that no longer persist in the colloquial, and to introduce words and meanings that are current nowadays though unknown to the classical written language. The same is true to some extent of grammatical forms and syntax.

The modern literary language, then, reflects an earlier stage, with the form of words fixed by written tradition, just as English spelling is. It is much as though Shakespearian English, with an admixture of Chaucerian and modern words, were the medium of written communication today. For example, the modern dative ending *-də* continues to be written in the older form *-dur*; the word *dolōn*, seven, which lost its intervocalic *γ* centuries ago, is still written in the uncontracted form *doloγan*, much as English 'eight' retains the old *gh* (still heard, however, in German or Dutch *acht*).

The classical (literary) language is to be the subject of study in these pages.

Modern Dialects

The Mongolian language is divided into a number of dialects, all sharing the same general grammatical and syntactical features, and more or less mutually comprehensible in spite of phonetic differences and developments. There is a large central group with four important dialects or groups of dialects, and three marginal dialects.

The Khalkha Mongolian dialect, comprising some 700,000 speakers in the MPR, as the language of a formally independent political unit and that with the greatest single number of speakers, may be regarded as the most important.

To the north of the centrally located Khalkha lies the Buryat Mongolian, whose speakers number 240,000, divided into the northern (cisbaikalian) and the southern (transbaikalian) divisions. South of Khalkha Mongolian, in the Chinese provinces of Inner Mongolia, are a number of dialects of which the Ordos and Chahar are best known. The Mongolian dialects of Manchuria are little investigated. Most of them belong together with the Ordos and Chahar to the South Mongolian group. The above comprise the eastern branch of Mongolian (Buryat in the north, Khalkha in the center, and Chahar and Ordos in the south).

The western branch of Mongolian is the Oirat dialect (generally called Kalmyk in Europe), spoken by some 130,000 persons. It is located far to the west in the former Kalmyk ASSR, west of the lower Volga at the north end of the Caspian sea. There are also speakers of Kalmyk in Sinkiang, Ch'ing-hai (in the Koko-Noor district), in Dzungaria (*jegün γar*, left hand) or West Mongolia, in Alashan and Edsin Gol.

In addition to these divisions, there are three isolated dialects. The Dagur is spoken in northern Manchuria, and has been influenced by Tungus. The Monguor (with related dialects) is spoken in the Kansu province of China, and in northeastern Tibet (Koko-Noor), and is strongly influenced by Chinese. The Mogul (Hazara and Aimak) is spoken in central Afghanistan northwest of Kabul.

Literature

The earliest Mongolian literary composition is an imperial chronicle, the so-called 'Secret History of the Mongols' (*mongγol-un niγuča tobčayan*), which may have been composed in the 13th century. Buddhist activity apparently set in under Qubilai Qagan, but the earliest translations of which we possess direct evidence date from the beginning of the 14th century. From that century we also possess a number of inscriptions but from following centuries only a trickle of documents on stone or paper has reached us.

A tremendous literary effort began shortly after 1600 when Legdan Qagan of the Chahars set his clergy the task of translating the whole of the Tibetan lamaistic canon, the Kanjur, into Mongolian. The literary Mongolian language of that translation (itself a faithful continuation of an unaltered tradition reaching back to the days of Chinggis Qagan) became, with slight modifications, the established norm for all later Mongolian literature.

The 17th, 18th and 19th centuries saw the production of a rich Buddhist and historical literature, the former culminating in the energetic printing activity in Peking in the 18th century, and the latter beginning about 1625 and continuing without interruption till the end of the 19th century. In this century the thread was again taken up, this time under Japanese auspices, only to be exploited later for the purposes of nationalistic propaganda.

The Mongolian Script

The alphabetic script of the Uighurs had been adopted by the Mongols as early as the time of Chinggis Qagan, and according to Mongol tradition, in 1204. The first known inscription dates from 1225, and there is definite evidence that before the middle of that century the Uighur script was used for literary compositions. In 1269 Qubilai Qagan authorized a modified form of the Tibetan script for use in Mongolian chancelleries (the ḥP'ags-pa or 'square' [*dörbeljin*] script). It continued in official use until about the middle of the 14th century, but was unable to compete with the much easier Uighur cursive script, which has remained in use until the present day.

For use among the Western Mongols, an improved form of the alphabet was devised in 1648. It is still used by the Kalmyks, the Mongols in the T'ien Shan in Sinkiang, and those in the Koko-Noor.

In the course of the 17th and 18th centuries the Mongolian alphabet adopted a few modifications from the Manchu alphabet. The Manchus had taken over the Mongolian script in 1599 and in 1632 submitted it to a process of revision and improvement, which benefited the Mongolian mother alphabet later.

The awakening of political consciousness in the last three decades was a thrust at the ancient tradition, and on Russian soil the link with the past through the Mongolian script was done away with at a stroke, when the Buryat Mongol ASSR adopted a modified Russian alphabet in 1937, and thus made literacy quickly available to all. In 1946, the Mongolian People's Republic followed suit. Books, periodicals and other writings are now apparently printed entirely in Cyrillic script. In essence, the dialects are now represented in writing as spoken.

II. Grammar

Lesson One

Contents. Alphabet and transcription; pronunciation; composition of words; accent; vowel harmony; parts of speech; gender; article.

§ 1. Alphabet and Transcription. The Mongolian alphabet, as here transcribed, consists basically of 23 letters: *a, b, č, d, e, g, γ, i, ǰ, k, l, m, n, o, ö, q, r, s, š, t, u, ü, y*.[1] Other transcriptions may employ somewhat different letters and use various diacritical marks, but these and other differences are slight, and will be readily understood by the student.

The Mongols themselves make no distinction between certain pairs of letters and use moreover the following order of letters: *a, e, i, o/u, ö/ü, n, q, γ, b, p, s, š, t/d, l, m, č, ǰ/y, k/g, r, v, h*. The three letters *v, h* and *p* occur solely in Chinese, Tibetan, Sanskrit and other foreign words.

§ 2a. Pronunciation. The letters *č, ǰ* and *š* may be pronounced as in English church, judge and show. The letter *γ* denotes an open back *g*, the voiced equivalent of the ch in German *acht*. The letter *q* originally denoted a velar (back) *k*, which in nearly all dialects has passed into the corresponding fricative *χ* (the unvoiced counterpart of *γ*). It may be pronounced in either manner. The remaining consonants have, roughly speaking, their normal English values.

In most modern dialects the vowels have been somewhat modified, varying according to dialect. *e, ö, ü* and sometimes also *i* are articulated with the middle part of the tongue, and *o* and *u* are pronounced with a marked narrowing of the articulating organs. For convenience they can be given their European values, with *ö* and *ü* as in German.

§ 2b. Composition of Words. The phonetic makeup of Mongolian words is simple, usually a regular alternation of vowels and consonants (*köbegün*, son). There are no initial or final consonant clusters, although two consonants may come together medially (*ülemǰi*, more). Mongolian has diphthongs in which the second element is *i* (mostly originating from an earlier *yi*, still reflected by the Mongolian script, but no longer recognized by the Mongols themselves) as in *sain* (from *sayin*) good, or *dalai*, sea. There is no notation for long vowels or consonants in the classical language. The few double letters seen are due to orthographical convention or hiatus.

---

[1] This is the order used in the lesson vocabularies. The glossary, however, uses a slightly different order.

Genuine Mongolian words may not begin with *l* or *r*, and may end only with *b*, *d*, *g*, *γ*, *l*, *m*, *n*, *r*, *s* and *š*. The presence of a following *i* causes *s* to become *š*. In manuscripts from South Mongolia *a* and *e* often become *i* after *č* and *ǰ*, especially in the second syllable, as in *üǰi-* for *üǰe-*, *čičeg* for *čečeg*.

§ 3. **Accent.** As a stress accent is not an integral part of the phonetic makeup of a word, the position of the accent may shift freely between syllables, and is phonologically irrevelant. For the purposes of reading a text in the classical language, however, the accent may be placed on the first syllable throughout.

§ 4. **Vowel Harmony.** The principle of vowel harmony is observed throughout the Mongolian language. Accordingly, the vowels in a word must all be front (or soft) vowels (*e*, *i*, *ö*, *ü*) or back (or hard) vowels (*a*, *i*, *o*, *u*). Note that *i* may occur in both series, probably because in the oldest language it had a velar counterpart (like the Turkish ı or the Russian jery) which later merged with *i*.
The vowel of the initial syllable determines whether the word will contain all front or all back vowels.

front	*köbegün*	son, boy
	ögülerün	saying
back	*qoyar*	two
	bayasqulang	gladness, rejoicing

Vowel harmony affects the velar consonants *k*/*g* as well, *k*/*g* being used with front vowels, and *q*/*γ* being required by back vowels.

aγula	mountain
degü	younger brother
bari-γ-ad	taking
üǰe-g-ed	seeing

As a result of vowel harmony, there are two forms for nearly every declensional and conjugational ending.

aγulan-dur	dative case (back)
degü-dür	dative case (front)
bariluya	perfect tense (back)
üǰelüge	perfect tense (front)

Labial harmony (whether rounded may follow unrounded vowels, or *vice versa*), such as in Turkish, is not observed in Classical Mongolian. All vowels may occur in all positions, but *o*/*ö* do not occur outside the first syllable (or in suffixes) unless *o*/*ö* are also in the first syllable. The vowels *a* and *u* are generally followed only by *a*, *u* or *i*, and likewise, *e* and *ü* by *e*, *ü* or *i*. *i* can be followed by all vowels except *o*/*ö*.

§ 5. **Parts of Speech.** The three main categories of speech are the noun, verb and indeclinables. There is no difference in form between adjectives and nouns, and no fundamental difference between these and the pronouns, although pronouns have certain characteristics of their own. Verbs may be formed from nouns, and nouns formed from verbs, but the stems thus produced are then one or the other. Some adverbs are in reality case forms of nouns, and many postpositions derive from nouns. Interjections, conjunctions and certain functional particles (as interrogative and negative) are indeclinable.

§ 6. **Gender.** Mongolian nouns have no grammatical gender. Sex is expressed only in the inherent meaning of the word, which fact plays no rôle in declension.

§ 7. **Article.** The Mongolian word *nigen*, one, is used as an indefinite article, and may occur before or after another adjective.

nigen yeke aɣula }
yeke nigen aɣula }   a large mountain

teimü nigen ɣajar-a   in such and such a place

There is no definite article.

Vocabulary 1

NB. The first occurrence of a word is entered in the vocabulary to that lesson. Verbs are entered by their stem form, followed by a dash. A few words are given on second occurrence.

aɣula(n)[1] mountain
bari- to take
bayasqulang gladness, rejoicing
čečeg flower
dalai sea
degü younger brother
eme female, woman
ɣajar land, country, place
köbegün son, boy

nige(n) one, a
ögüle- to say
qaɣan king, Khan
qoyar two
sain good
teimü such, such a
üje- to see
ülemji more
yeke large, great

Lesson Two

Contents. Cases; nominative; nominative particles; genitive; accusative; word order. Reading exercise (1).

§ 8. **Cases.** The noun in classical Mongolian is declined in seven cases: nominative, genitive, accusative, dative-locative, ablative, instrumental and comitative (also called sociative). Of these, the first three are

---

[1] For an explanation of words in -(n), see Lesson Three, § 18.

syntactic in their functions, while the remainder all indicate spatial and other notional relationships.

The same set of endings is used for adjectives, nouns, pronouns and verbal nouns alike.

It is an orthographical convention of Mongolian to write declensional and certain other endings as a separate word, which avoids disturbing a familiar word picture in the original script. In transcription these elements are separated by a dash.

§ 9. **Nominative.** The nominative case is the case of the subject, and displays the stem form of the noun. Sentences with verbs of predication have the subject in the nominative case.

yeke ayula bülüge.	It was a large mountain.
yayun bui?	What is it?
bars yayun idemüi?	What does a tiger eat?
ene bülüge.	That was it.

§ 10. **Nominative particles.** The nominative is often denoted by the particle *ber*, which emphasizes the preceding word (much like Turkish *da, de* or Russian *že*) and indicates that that word is the subject. Its origin lies in an ergative construction (note *infra*, Lesson Three, § 16, the similarity to the instrumental ending *-bar/-ber*).

odqan köbegün ber bars-i üjebei.	The youngest son saw the tiger.

In the primitive form, this would be rendered somewhat as follows: "By the youngest son seeing was performed with respect to the tiger."

The particles *inu* and *anu* are of similar function. They owe their origin to the genitive forms of **i*, he, and **a*, they (these nominative forms no longer exist), and function as a kind of definite article. Although they frequently retain the meaning 'his, their' in the classical language, the distinction between singular and plural is not observed.

basa qoyar aqa-nar anu ögülebei	Then { his / the } two elder brothers said:

§ 11. **Genitive.** Mongolian nouns in the genitive have the ending *-un/-ün* for stems ending in a consonant except *-n*, and the ending *-yin* for vowel stems. Stems in *-n*, however, take only *-u/-ü*.

ger house	*bars* tiger
ger-ün	*bars-un*
eke mother	*aqa* elder brother
eke-yin	*aqa-yin*
köbegün son	*qayan* king
köbegün-ü	*qayan-u*

The genitive plus the verb 'to be' is often used in the function of a verb 'to have'.

qayan-u yurban köbegün büliige.	The king's three sons were (or existed), *i.e.*, the king had three sons.

The genitive case always occurs before the element which it modifies.

§ 12. **Accusative.** The accusative is the normal case of the definite direct object. Its ending is *-i* after consonants, and *-yi* after vowels.

köbegün ber bars-i üjemüi.	The son sees the tiger.
ečige ber eke-yi asayubai.	The father asked the mother.

When the object is indefinite, the form coincides with the nominative, in the so-called absolute or indefinite case.

bars miqa idemüi.	A tiger eats meat (not a particular piece, but meat as a general practice).

The object stands in almost adverbial relation to the verb, and might be rendered literally by 'the tiger meat-eats'. If a specific piece of meat were meant (such as one mentioned previously), that would of course require the regular accusative.

bars ber miqa-yi idemüi.	The tiger eats the meat.

§ 13. **Word Order.** The essential order of words in the Mongolian sentence requires the subject to come first, and the verb last, while all other elements are arranged in between. Adjectival or attributive elements, including constructions with declined verbal nouns, precede the noun, and any object or complement precedes the verb.

yeke nigen bars ber		*oi-dur*	*oduysan*	A big tiger ate the king's
big a tiger nom. part.		in the woods	having gone	three sons, who
qayan-u yurban köbegün-i	*idebei.*			had gone into
king's three sons (acc.)	ate			the woods.

Reading Exercise (1)

NB. Owing to the connected thought of this and later reading selections, it is necessary to present some forms not yet discussed in the grammar. These are explained in accompanying notes.

nigen yajar-tur[1] *qayan qatun qoyar*[2] *büliige. tere qayan-u yurban köbegün*[3] *büliige. yurban köbegün-ü ečige ber qayan büliige. köbegün-ü eke ber qatun büliige. eke-yin yurban köbegün büliige. qayan yurban*

---

[1] *nigen yajar-tur* is in the dative case: 'in a (certain) country'.
[2] *qayan qatun qoyar*, lit. 'king queen two', or 'king and queen'.
[3] *yurban köbegün*, 'three sons'. The presence of a qualifying number makes a plural ending unnecessary.

köbegün-i bariyad[4], *oi ayulan-dur*[5] *odbai. ayula yeke büliige. yeke*
5 *ayula büliige. nigen bars oi-ača*[6] *yaruyad*[7], *yurban köbegün-dür irebei.*
odqan köbegün ber bars-i üjeged, ögülerün[8], *'oi-dur olan bars*[9] *buyu.*
bars yayun idemüi?', ögülebei. yeke köbegün ber odqan köbegün-dür
ögülerün, 'bars miqa čisu[10] *idemüi', ögülebei. odqan köbegün asayurun*[11],
'bars-un miqa ken idemüi?', ögülebei.

Vocabulary 2

-ača/-eče ablative case	*yar-* to come out
anu nominative particle	*yurban* three
aqa elder brother	*ide-* to eat
asayu- to ask	*inu* nominative particle
-bai/-bei preterite tense	*ire-* to come
bars tiger	*ken* who
basa then	*miqa(n)* meat, flesh
ber nominative particle	*-mui/-müi* present tense
bui, buyu is, there is (present tense)	*-nar/-ner* plural ending
büliige was, there was (perfect tense)	*od-* to go, proceed
čisu(n) blood	*odqan* youngest
-dur/-dür dative case	*oi* woods, forest
ečige father	*olan* many, much, very
eke mother	*qatun* queen
ene this	*-run/-rün* verbal ending
ger tent, house, home	*tere* that
-yad/-ged verbal ending (see notes)	*-tur* see *-dur*
	yayun what?

Lesson Three

Contents. Dative-locative; ablative; instrumental; comitative; variable *-n* stems; nominal inflection table; reflexive forms of nouns. Reading exercise (2).

§ 14. Dative-locative. The dative case has the usual 'to, for' meanings, and incorporates as well the 'in' meaning of the locative. It has the endings *-tur/-tür.* After vowels, *m, n,* and *l,* the ending is *-dur/-dür.*

---

[4] *bariyad* is a verbal form coordinate with the finite form *odbai,* he went. It may be translated 'taking his ... he went ...' or 'he took ... and went ...'.
[5] *oi ayulan-dur,* 'to the woods and mountains, or to the wooded mountain (i.e., out in the wilds)'. The case ending may refer to both words, or the first word may qualify the second.
[6] *oi-ača* is in the ablative case: 'from the woods'.
[7] *yaruyad* is the same construction as in Note 4.
[8] *ögülerün* may be translated for the time being as 'saying'. Its value is little more than that of introductory quotation marks.
[9] *olan bars,* 'many tigers'. Expressions of plurality do not generally require the plural ending.
[10] *miqa čisu.* Supply 'and' to make it 'flesh and blood'.
[11] *asayurun* may be translated as 'asked'.

nigen γaǰar-tur	in a (certain) country
tere čay-tur	at that time, then
tere ǰüg-tür	in that direction, that way
oi-dur odbai.	He went to the woods.

Another form of the dative is in *-a / -e*, and is mostly encountered in older texts. It is often used to prevent a tiresome repetition of *dur, dur*. The spoken language has *-d(ə)*, which goes back to still another suffix *-da / -de*, which also may be met with occasionally in literary Mongolian. By way of compromise many recent MSS write *-du / -dü*.

§ 15. **Ablative.** The ablative case, which ends in *-ača / -eče*, has the meaning 'from', and is also used in expressions of comparison.

oi-ača	from the woods
qola-ača	from afar
ger-eče	from the tent
nada-ača küčütei bolbasu	if he be stronger than I

§ 16. **Instrumental.** The instrumental case expresses 'by means of, with, for', and has the endings *-iyar / -iyer* after a consonant, and *-bar / -ber* after a vowel.

öber-ün čisun-iyar	with his own blood
üčügen üne-ber	for a low price
modu-bar, modun-iyar	with a stick, by means of a club

§ 17. **Comitative.** The comitative case (also called the sociative case) is the case of accompaniment, 'with, together with, in the company of', and has the endings *-luγa / -lüge*.

aqa-luγa	with (his) older brother
ečige-lüge	with father
altan-luγa adali	similar to gold

§ 18. **Variable -*n* Stems.** Nouns ending in *-n* are of two types: stable *-n* stems and variable *-n* stems. The former, as the name indicates, retain the *-n* in all cases. In the latter type, the nominative and the definite accusative may retain *-n* or may lose it, and the indefinite loses it, while the instrumental may use either stem.

Apart from this, however, is the fact that nouns ending in *-n* generally lose this consonant when a suffix beginning with a consonant is added, e.g., *γurban*, three, but *γurbaγula*, the three of them (< *γurban* + *γula*).

aγulan-dur odbai.	He went to the mountain.
bars ber miqa-yi idemüi.	The tiger eats the meat.
bars (ber) miqa idemüi.	A tiger eats meat.
modu-yi } *baribai* *modun-i*	He seized the club.
modu-bar } *bars-i alabai.* *modun-iyar*	He killed the tiger with a club.

2 *

§ 19. **Nominal Inflection Table.** We now may regard the complete picture of nominal inflection.

NOMINAL INFLECTION TABLE

Case	Consonant Stem		Vowel Stem		-n Stem[1]	
	back	front	back	front	stable front	variable back
Nom.	čay	ger	aqa	eke	köbegün	modu(n)
Gen.	čay-un	ger-ün	aqa-yin	eke-yin	köbegün-ü	modun-u
Acc.	čay-i	ger-i	aqa-yi	eke-yi	köbegün-i	modu-yi / modun-i
Dat.-Loc.	čay-tur / čay-a	ger-tür / ger-e	aqa-dur	eke-dür	köbegün-dür / köbegün-e	modun-dur / modun-a
Ablat.	čay-ača	ger-eče	aqa-ača	eke-eče	köbegün-eče	modun-ača
Instr.	čay-iyar	ger-iyer	aqa-bar	eke-ber	köbegün-iyer	modun-iyar / modu-bar
Comit.	čay-luya	ger-lüge	aqa-luya	eke-lüge	köbegün-lüge	modun-luya

[1] Both front and back words may be stable or variable

§ 20. **Reflexive Forms of Nouns.** Mongolian expresses the reflexive pronominal adjective 'one's own' by a reflexive suffix added after the declensional suffix, which in the gen., acc. and dat. cases may assume a different form. These forms always refer back to the subject of the sentence, *i.e.*, our (own) father, his (own) tent. The basic endings are *-iyan/-iyen* after a consonant, and *-ban/-ben* or *-γan/-gen* after a vowel. These endings may in themselves serve as the genitive and accusative forms. The genitive and dative also have some anomalous forms.

aqa degü qoyar bars-i ečige-		The elder and younger brother
-dür-iyen ögbei.		gave the tiger to their (own) father.

Gen. ⎫	*qaγan-yuγan*	*eke-yügen*
	qaγan-(y)uban	*eke-yüben*
Acc. ⎭	*qaγan-iyan*	*eke-ben*
Dat.-Loc.	*qaγan-dur-iyan*	*eke-dür-iyen*
	qaγan-daγan	*eke-degen*
Ablat.	*qaγan-ačaγan*	*eke-ečegen*
	qaγan-ačaban	*eke-ečeben*
Instr.	*qaγan-iγar-iyan*	*eke-ber-iyen*
Comit.	*qaγan-luγa-ban*	*eke-lüge-ben*

Reading Exercise (2)

odqan köbegün ber aqa-luγa oi-ača γaruγad, qaγan ečige-dür irebei.
odqan köbegün ber bars-i üjeged, aqa-daγan ögülerün, 'oi-dur bars
üjeged, bars-i alamui¹', kemen² ögülebei. aqa ber degü-ben bariγad,
oi-ača γaruγad ger-tegen irebei. aqa degü qoyar modu-bar bars alaγad,
5 *bars-i ečige-dür-iyen ögbei. qaγan bars-i yeke dura-bar bariγad, γurban*
köbegün-iyen eke qatun-dur ögbei.

Vocabulary 3

adali like, similar	*keme-* to say
ala- to kill	*küčütei* strong
alta(n) gold	*modu(n)* tree, wood, stick
bolbasu if, if it be	*nada-* stem of *bi* I
čaγ time	*öber* oneself
dura(n) desire, pleasure	*ög-* to give
γurban three	*qola* far, distant
γurbaγula a group of three	*üčügen* little, small
jüg direction, side	*üne* price, value

---

¹ *bars-i alamui*, lit. 'seeing a tiger ..., we kill ...' (the subject 'we' is drawn from the context), and freely, 'when we see a tiger in the woods, we (habitually) kill the tiger'.

² *kemen.* Translate 'saying'. Its value here is that of closing quotation marks (equals Turkish *diye*).

Lesson Four

Contents. Adjectives and comparison of adjectives; adjectival suffixes; avoidance of ambiguity; formation of plurals; the verb; durative; preterite; coördinative gerund. Reading Selections: I. The Fool
and the Sandalwood. II. The Ass in the Panther's Skin.

NB. Owing to the length of Lesson Four, two study periods are best
devoted to it.

§ 21 a. **Adjectives.** There is no formal difference between adjectives and
nouns. A noun placed before another noun functions as an attribute
to the latter. Thus, *altan* means 'gold', but in the nominal group *altan
ordu*, 'the golden horde', it is an attribute.

ünen	true, truth, truly
qara	black, the black, that which is black
qara morin	a black horse
yeke	big, large, greatly, greatness, size
yeke eljige	a large donkey
yeke idebei.	it ate a great deal; it ate much.

§ 21 b. **Comparison of Adjectives.** In compensation for the absence of
comparison of adjectives as known in Western languages, the meaning
of an adjective may be reinforced or underlined by words like *maši*,
very, *ülemji*, more, *bügüde*, every, or *qamuy*, all. The last two words
require the genitive or ablative case.

maši yeke	very large, larger
ülemji yeke	larger, greater
ülemji bayan	richer
qamuy-ača küčütü	strongest (of all)
qamuy-un degere	highest (of all)

As in Turkic languages, certain adjectives may form an intensifying
prefix from their initial syllable + -*b*, which imparts the meaning 'the
highest degree of' to the adjective.

sab sain	the very best
qab qara	pitch black
čab čayan	snow white
šib šine	brand new

§ 22. **Adjectival Suffixes.** The derivative suffix -*tu* / -*tü* (alternate form
-*tai* / -*tei*) means 'having, possessed of', and often has adjectival significance. -*n* generally is lost before this ending.

morin	horse
moritu	horse owner, a rider
üne	price, value
üne-tü	having value, valuable
usun	water
usu-tu quduy	a water-filled well

A faint trace of an old Mongolian formal distinction between masculine and feminine is displayed in this suffix. Older classical texts (usually from the 17th century) differentiate *-tu / -tü* for masculine and *-tai / -tei* for feminine. Later texts use both forms indiscriminately but with a decided preference for *-tu / -tü*.

In the modern language the suffix *-tai / -tei* develops into a new comitative case, displacing *-luγa / -lüge*.

Adjectives of color qualifying a feminine noun take the suffix *-γčin / -gčin*.

ölögčin	female, female being
ölögčin bars	female tiger, tigress
qara morin	black stallion
qaraγčin morin	black mare
čaγaγčin morin	white mare

§ 23. **Avoidance of ambiguity.** Declensional endings are generally added only to the last word in a series. In cases where the first word could conceivably be construed as belonging to a series, the presence of an intercalated nominative particle such as *ber* will indicate the subject. Furthermore, adjectival function arising from juxtaposition of nouns may make possible two slightly different renderings of a phrase. However, the use of the reflexive forms of nouns prevents ambiguities such as that in English sentences like "He gave him his book".

aγula oi-dur odbai.	He went to the mountain and the woods, or, to the mountainous woods.
oi aγulan-dur odbai.	He went to the woods and the mountains, or, to the wooded mountains.
bars miqa idemüi.	He eats tiger('s) meat, or, A tiger eats meat.
bars ber miqa idemüi.	A tiger eats meat.
bars ber miqa-yi idemüi.	The tiger eats the meat.
bars-un miqa-yi idemüi.	He eats the meat of a tiger.
köbegün ber eke-yi asaγubai.	The son asked his mother.
köbegün eke-yi asaγubai.	He asked his son and mother (someone else's).
köbegün eke-ben asaγubai.	He asked his (own) son and mother.
köbegün-ü eke-yi asaγubai.	He asked the son's mother.

§ 24. **Formation of Plurals.** Plural formation in Mongolian is not such a vital topic as in some other languages, as the mere presence of a quantity word is sufficient indication of plurality. As a rule, the specific plural suffixes are resorted to only in cases of ambiguity. Thus they rarely occur after quantity words such as numerals. In most cases the

indication of the category suffices and the exact interpretation in terms
of number is left to the reader.

γurban köbegün	three sons
olan bars	many tigers

The plural is formed by adding one of various suffixes, after which
the regular case endings may be added. The suffixes most often used
are the following.

a) *-nar / -ner* is a plural indicating a group of individuals, or a circle
of similar people.

aqa-nar	the elder brothers (sons of one father)
tengri-ner	the gods (of a pantheon)

b) *-čud / -čüd* is a plural for human beings.

mongγolčud	the Mongols
bayačud	the children (as of one clan)

c) *-s* is of purely plural significance and may be used for all vowel stems.

üge-s	words
tengri-s	gods (in general)
aqa-s	elder brothers (in the sense of 'the older generation')

The *-i* of words in *-oi* or *-ai* drops before *-s*.

noqai	*noqas*	dogs
moγai	*moγas*	snakes

d) *-d* is used for vowel stems, or stems in *-l, -n, -r*. Stems in *-sun / -sün*
drop this suffix entirely.

qaγan	*qaγad*	kings, qagans
qan	*qad*	minor princes
noyan	*noyad*	noblemen, princes
tüšimel	*tüšimed*	minister
balγasun	*balγad*	city

Stems in other consonants intercalate the vowel *-u- / -ü-* before the *-d*.

čerig	*čerig-ü-d*	soldiers

e) The plural ending *-nuγud / -nügüd* may be added to words as a
strengthener.

jaγan-nuγud	elephants, elephant herd
olan-nuγud	very many, all

Mongolian sometimes uses a double plural formation.

lama-nar-ud	lamas, priests
bayadud	children
noyadud	princes
qaγadud	kings, qagans

The derivative forms in *-tu | -tü* and *-tai | -tei* form their plural in *-tan | -ten.*

amin	life
amitu	one alive, a being
amitan	living being(s)
moritan	horsemen

§ 25. **The Verb.** The Mongolian verb does not distinguish person, gender or number. The subject of a verb is to be seen from the subject of the sentence, or, if that remains unexpressed, from the context. The different verb forms are formed by means of suffixes. Some of those beginning with a consonant intercalate an *-u- | -ü-* after a final stem consonant. This is indicated in the following by *u* or *ü* in parentheses.

§ 26. **Durative.** The durative form, corresponding in many respects to the present tense of Western languages, is indicated by *-(u)mui |* *-(ü)müi* added to the stem. This form is general, but used concretely. It also occurs in the use of an historical present.

abumui	he takes
idemüi	he eats

Some older alternate forms still occur sporadically, chiefly that in *-m*, as *abum*, or *-nam*, as *bainam*, is.

§ 27. **Preterite.** The preterite in *-bai | -bei* (after *b* and *r* with intercalated *u*) is used to depict in a factual manner an event which is finished, or the occurrences in a narrative.

ögbei	he gave
abubai	he took
idebei	he ate

A preterite ending in *-ba | -be* is also found.

§ 28. **The Coördinative Gerund.** The form in *-(u)γad | -(ü)ged* may be termed a coördinative gerund, or a gerund of parallel action. When two actions on a par with each other are expressed in the same sentence, the first will occur in the *-γad | -ged* form, while the second will have a finite form such as *-mui* or *-bai* (which in its turn may again be replaced by a gerund etc.). It is best translated by two finite forms. The negation is *ülü.*

abuγad	taking, when he took
ideged	eating, when he ate
qaγan γurban köbegün-i ba-riγad, oi-dur odbai.	Taking his three sons, the king went to the wood. OR: The king took his three sons and went to the wood.

Reading Selections

I. The Fool and the Sandalwood[*]

*nigen teneg kümün ber altan-luya adali üne-tü goršiša neretü čandan
modun-i oluyad, qudalduyan-u yajar-a abču oduysan-dur*[1] *ken ber*[2] *ču
ese abubai. tegünče nigen negüresün qudalduyči-luya qamtu qonoyad,
tegün-ü negüresün-i ulus abuysan-i üjejü*[3] *'ene arya sain' kemen sanayad,*
5 *čandan-iyan tülejü*[4] *negüresün bolyayad, maši üčügen üne-ber qudalduluya*[5].

II. The Ass in the Panther's Skin[**]

nigen arya-tu kümün ber eljigen-degen irbis-ün ‖ *arasun-i emüskeged
busud-un tariyan-a talbiysan-dur*[1] *ulus ber 'tariyan-dur irbis orojuqui*[2]*'
kemejü*[3] *ayuyad ese kögebei. tegün-eče ulam yeke ideküi-dür*[4] *olan ulus*
10 *čuylayad qola-ača qarbuju alabasu*[5] *tere inu arya-tu kümün-ü eljige
ajuyu*[6].

Vocabulary 4

ab- to take, to buy
ajuyu there was
ami(n) life
  amitan being, creature
  amitu one alive, a being
arasu(n) skin, hide

arya plan, trick
  arya-tu crafty
ayu- to fear, dread
baya small
  bayačud children
baina(m) is (durative of 'to be')

Selection I.
* From the commentary to the *Subhāṣitaratnanidhi* by Sa-skya paṇḍita
(1182—1251), titled in Mongolian *saitur nomlaysan erdeni-yin sang
subašidi kemekü šastir*, a xylograph (56 by 17 cm.), not dated, of 198
folios, in the Mongolian collection of The Royal Library, Copenhagen.
Short title, and reference: *Subhāṣita* 5, fol. 4 v.

[1] *abču oduysan-dur*, 'when he took it, and went out to ...'.
[2] *ken ber*, Adding *ber* to *ken*, 'who', makes the indefinite pronoun, 'whoever'.
ču is emphatic. Lit. 'whoever it may be did not buy it', i.e., no one at
all bought it.
[3] *ulus abuysan-i üjejü*, 'when he saw people buy ...'.
[4] *tülejü*, translate as 'burning'.
[5] *qudalduluya*, 'he sold (it)', is in the perfect tense.

Selection II.
** *Subhāṣita* 6, fol. 2 v.

[1] *talbiysan-dur*, 'when he sent out his ...'.
[2] *orojuqui*, translate as 'is loose'.
[3] *kemejü*, translate as 'saying'.
[4] *yeke ideküi-dür*, 'because it had eaten greatly'.
[5] *qarbuju alabasu*, 'shooting ... they killed (it)'.
[6] *ajuyu*, translate as 'being'. 'It being the crafty man's ...' or freely,
'and it was only the crafty man's donkey'.

balyasun city, town
bol- to be
  bolya- to make
busu other, different; not
bügüde all
čayan white
čandan sandalwood
čerig soldier
ču emphatic particle
čuyla- to assemble, gather
degere high, upper, above
eljige(n) ass, donkey
emüske- to dress (tr.)
ese no, not
goršiša a type of sandalwood
irbis panther
jayan elephant
köge- to hunt, rout out
kümün man
lama priest, lama
-luya perfect tense ending
maši very, more
moyai snake, serpent
mongyol Mongol, Mongolian
mori(n) horse
  moritu rider, horseman
negüresün charcoal
nere name
  neretü named, called
noqai dog
noyan prince, lord
ol- to find, acquire
ordu(n) camp, palace
oro- to go in, enter
ölögčin female being

qamtu (postposed, with comitative) together
qamuy all
qan minor prince, lord
qara black
qarbu- to shoot (with bow and arrow)
qono- to stay, dwell (overnight)
qudaldu- to sell
  qudalduyan sale, trade
  qudalduyči seller, merchant
quduy well
sain good, fine
sana- to think, recall
šine new
talbi- to put, place; to release, abandon
tariya(n) field, meadow
teneg foolish
tengri (or *tngri*), god, heaven
tere this
  tegün- oblique stem of *tere*
  tegünče then, thereupon (from ablative)
tüle- to burn
tüšimel minister, official
ulam gradually
ulus people, nation
usun water
  usu-tu watery, water-filled
üge word, speech
ülemji more
üne price, value
  üne-tü valuable
üne(n) truth

Lesson Five

Contents. Gerunds (in *-n*, *-ču/-ju*); verbal nouns (in *-qu/-kü*, *-yči* and *-ysan*); declension of verbal nouns. Reading Selection: III. The Timid Hares.

§ 29. **Gerunds.** Gerunds (also called **converbs**) are unvarying verbal forms, not declined or conjugated, which indicate ties between actions and various degrees of subordination.

a) The **gerund of absolute subordination** ends in *-(u)n/-(ü)n*.

  abun   *iden*

It indicates an action completely subordinate to the following form, which may be another gerund or a finite form. The negation is *ülü*.

üjen oduɣad saɣun büküi- *-dür* . . .	'looking, (they) went out; sitting, (they) were', *i.e.*, they went out and looked, and while they were sitting there . . .

Its most frequent use is in the word *kemen*, 'saying', now reduced to the value of mere quotation marks.

b) The **subordinate gerund** ends in *-ču / -čü* after consonants (except *l*) and in *-ǰu / -ǰü* after vowels and *l*.

abču   *ideǰü*

The action expressed by the subordinate gerund must logically occur before that in the form to which it is subordinate. It is consequently best translated into English by a separate clause. The negation is *ülü*.

qola-ača qarbuǰu alabasu	When they killed it, by shooting from afar . . .
čandan-iyan tüleǰü negüresün bolɣaɣad . . . qudalduluya.	After making charcoal, by burning his sandalwood, he sold it . . .

c) The **coördinative gerund** in *-ɣad / -ged* has been treated above (Lesson Four, § 28).

§ 30. Verbal Nouns. A verbal noun is a substantive derived from a verb. It may act as a verb with regard to what precedes it, but is inflected like any other noun. Several verbal nouns are frequently used as predicates and thus enter on a line with the finite verbal forms.

a) The **infinitive** (also called **future participle**), or *nomen abstractum*, is used in a purely abstract sense, or for an action not seen concretely. It denotes the concept of the action indicated by the verb. It ends in *-qu / -kü* or *-qui / -küi*.

abqu	the taking (Ger. das Nehmen), that which one takes
ideküi	the eating (Ger. das Essen), that which one eats
ta aɣuqu kereg ügei.	Your fearing (is) without reason.
šal kemekü daɣun	a sound saying 'splash'

Furthermore, it is used as a finite form with future meaning.

či maɣad ükükü.	You will surely die.

It may take the negatives *ügei* or *ülü*.
There is an archaic plural form in *-qun / -kün*.

aqun	those who are, live
bükün	those who exist; everything

Lesson Five 25

b) The **present participle**, or *nomen actoris*, ends in *-(u)yči|-(ü)gči*, and since it is concrete, denoting a real thing, it may have a plural, which is in *-d* (archaic plural in *-n*). The negation is *ülü*.

abuyči	he who is taking, the taking one
idegči	he who is eating, the eating one
qudalduyči	the seller, merchant
šal kemegči yayun bui?	What is that which says 'splash'?

c) The **preterite participle**, or *nomen concretum*, describes a concrete action or the concrete result of an action. It ends in *-(u)ysan|-(ü)gsen*. Its plural is in *-d* (before which *-n* disappears), *-(u)ysad|-(ü)gsed*. The negations are *ügei* or *ülü*.

abuysan	he who has taken, that which has been taken
idegsen	he who has eaten, that which has been eaten
abuysad	the taken things, those things one has taken
qamiya iregsen bui?	'Where is it having come?', i.e., Where did it come from?
bi sonosuysan büliige.	I am one having heard (it); I am the one who heard it.
qamuy-i daruysan bayatur.	The hero who has conquered everything.

§ 31. **Declension of Verbal Nouns.** Being nouns, these forms may have plurals (except for the abstract infinitive), and be declined according to their use in the sentence. Since person is not expressed in a form like *kemeküi-dür*, lit. 'in the saying', it may be drawn from the subject, 'he', 'in his saying', i.e., when he said.

a) **Genitive.**

teimü nigen yajar-a ireküi-yin čimege-yi bi sonosuysan büliige.	I am the one who heard a noise come to such and such a place.
jimis unaqu-yin dayun	the noise of fruit falling

b) **Accusative.**

dayun yarqu-yi taulai sonosuyad	When the hares heard the sound coming out (resounding)

c) **Locative.** The literal meaning of 'in, in that' can often be translated by 'when'.

ünege ber 'yayun bui' kemeküi-dür	When the fox said 'What is that?'
čandan-i abču oduysan-dur	When he went out, taking the sandalwood

d) **Ablative.** This may be translated by 'from, since, because of' and
so on.

kedün taulai aysan-ača	From there being some hares, or, since there were some hares ...
arsalan taulai qoyar qamtu baiysan-ača	Because of a lion's being together with a hare ...

e) **Instrumental.** This is most often used with the form in *-ysan*, which
combines with the ending *-yar* (an alternate form of *-bar*) to yield
-ysayar / -gseger. It may be translated 'while, by, owing to, what with'
and so forth.

maši olan küriiged ayun du-tayaysayar ...	Owing to the coming of a great many who had become frightened and fled ...
kürkü-ber	in order to arrive

f) **Comitative.**

qudalduyči-luya	with a merchant
bolyaqui-luya qamtuda	in addition to making ...

Reading Selection

III. The Timid Hares*

urida nigen nayur-un dergede kedün taulai aysan-ača usun-u köbege-deki[1]
modun-u ǰimis nayur-tur unaqui-dur šal kemekü dayun yarqu-yi taulai
sonosuyad ayuǰu dutayayad ünegen-e učiraysan-dur ünege ber 'yayun
bui' kemekiii-dür, taulai ber 'šal irebei' kemegsen-dür ünege basa du-
5 *tayabai[2]. tere metü ulamǰilan sonosuyad maši olan küriiged ayun*
dutayaysayar, nigen arsalan-dur kürčü ögülegsen-dür arsalan ber 'šal
kemegči yayun bui, qamiya iregsen bui' kemekiii-dür, tedeger[3] ber öber
öberün[4] ken-eče sonosuysan-iyan dam dam asayuysayar, taulai-dur
tulqui-dur taulai ber 'teimü nigen yaǰar-a irekiii-yin čimege-yi bi
10 *sonosuysan büliige' kemeged bügüde-yi dayayulǰu, tere nayur-un ǰaqa-dur*
küriiged küliyeǰü baitala[5], nigen ǰimis unayad šal geǰü dayun yaruysan-
-dur, taulai ber 'ene büliige' kemebei. tegün-e arsalan ber 'ene inu ǰimis
unaqu-yin dayun bui-ǰa. ta ayuqu kereg ügei' kemeǰü bügüde-yi amu-
yululuya[6].

---

* *Subhāṣita 5, fol. 5 r.*

[1] *köbege-deki*, 'at the edge of'.

[2] This first sentence is not long by Mongolian standards. The student
may compare his translation with that given in Lesson Six, § 32.

[3] *tedeger*, or *tede*, is the nom. pl. of the demonstrative pronoun *tere*, this
(gen. *tegün-ü*, etc.).

[4] *öber öberün ken-eče*, 'from whom they themselves (had heard it)'.

[5] *baitala*. Translate 'while they stood (and waited)'.

[6] *amuyululuya*. The perfect tense in *-luya* is used to conclude a narrative.

Vocabulary 5

a- to be
amuγul- to calm (trans.)
arsalan lion
bai- to be; to stand
bi I
bü- to be, to exist
či thou, you (2nd p. sg.)
čimege sound, noise
daγa- to follow
daγaγul- to cause to follow after
daγu(n) sound, noise
dam dam one after the other
daru- to press, conquer
dergede beside; towards; before
dutaγa- to flee
ge- to say
-ǰa indeed, to be sure
ǰaqa edge, shore
ǰimis fruit, berries
kedün some, several
kereg cause, matter, reason
köbege edge, border
küliye- to wait

kür- to come, to arrive
maγad surely, certainly
metü postposition, like
naγur lake
öber self, oneself
qamiγa where
qamtuda = qamtu postp., together
saγu- to sit, dwell
sonos- to hear
šal 'splash' (onomatapoetic)
ta you (2nd p. pl.)
taulai hare
tedeger these (pl. of *tere*)
tegün- oblique of *tere*
tul- to get to, to reach
učira- to meet
ulamǰilan gradually
una- to fall
urida previously, once
ügei postposition, without
ükü- to die
ülü particle, no, not
ünege(n) fox

Lesson Six

Contents. Style; remaining finite forms (in *-luγa*, *-ǰuqui*, and *-yu*); remaining gerunds (reporting, purpose, condition, terminative). Reading Selection: IV. The Lion and the Hare.

§ 32. **Style.** Mongolian documents in the 17th century still retain a terse direct style of reporting, reflecting no doubt the oral style of narration. Towards the end of the 17th century, however, it became fashionable and elegant to extend sentences to great lengths by substituting gerunds for finite forms and otherwise prolonging the thought. In fact, the longer the sentence, the more literary was considered to be the style. An early text displaying this tendency is the Chronicle of Saγang Sečen (also called Sanang Sečen) dating from 1662. The new style arose under the influence of literary Tibetan. In English, of course, these involved constructions must be broken up into smaller parts, with generous use of clauses.

Sample sentence.	Literal translation.
urida nigen naγur-un dergede kedün taulai aγsan-ača usun--u köbege-deki modun-u ǰimis naγur-tur unaqui-dur šal ke-	Once upon a time, owing to some hares living beside a lake, the hares, hearing a noise resound, saying 'splash', of fruit from a tree

mekü dayun γarqu-yi taulai	at the water's edge falling into the
sonosuyad ayuju dutayayad	lake, becoming frightened and
ünegen-e učiraysan-dur ünege	fleeing, and having met a fox, and
ber 'yaγun bui' kemeküi-dur,	the fox having said, "What is it?",
taulai ber 'šal irebei' kemeg-	and the hares saying, "A noise
sen-dür ünege basa dutayabai.	came", the fox fled thereupon.

Literary translation

Once upon a time, there were some hares who lived beside a lake. Fruit from a tree at the water's edge fell into the lake. The hares, when they heard a sound saying 'splash' resound, became frightened and fled. They met a fox, who said, "What is it?" The hares said, "A noise came." The fox thereupon fled.

The following sentence is a good illustration of the use of the various subordinating gerunds[1].

bi morin-i aqa-ača erin abču	I went and got the horse from my
degü-degen ögüged, tere inu	elder brother and gave it to my
tegün-i nada-ača abču, bi	younger brother, who took it from
aryamji abura ger dotora oro-	me and while I went into the tent
tala, degü ber ken-dür yaγun-i	to get a rope, younger brother, not
ču ögülel ügegüye mordoju	saying anything to anyone, went
odbai.	riding off.

§ 33. **Remaining Finite Forms.**

a) **Perfect.** The perfect tense ends in *-(u)luya/-(ü)lüge.*

abuluya	he has taken
idelüge	he has eaten

This states a fact of completed action, and the situation thus established. It is often found on the closing verb in a narration (*cf.* texts to date).

Dharma-bala-yi qaγan bolya-luya.	They have made Dharma-bala king.

b) **Verb** in *-čuqui/-čüküi (-juqui/-jüküi* after vowels and *-l*). This form gives objective statements about the general state of affairs at a given moment. It may not occur with the first person.

abčuqui	
idejüküi	
tariyan-dur irbis orojuqui.	A panther has got loose on the fields.
tere tüšimel ese boljuqui.	He did not become his minister.
ireged üjeged deilejüküi.	*Veni, vidi, vici.*

---

[1] From I. J. Schmidt, *Grammatik der mongolischen Sprache*, St. Petersburg, 1831, p. 65.

Lesson Six 29

c) **Verb** in *-(u)yu / -(ü)yü.* This form is used in general statements which are valid irrespective of time.

abuyu
ideyü
nigültü kilinča üiledbesü, ami-   If living beings commit sinful
tan tamu-dur unayu.   acts, they fall into hell.

§ 34. Remaining Gerunds.

a) **Gerund of Reporting.** Verbs of saying, speaking, *etc.* (*verba declarandi*), have a special form to introduce direct speech. It ends in *-(u)run / -(ü)rün.*

ögülerün   (thus) saying
asayurun   inquiring (as follows)
jarliy bolurun   commanding, declaiming (of royal
     personages, 'saying')

b) **Gerund of Purpose.** Intention or purpose is expressed by the ending *-(u)ra / -(ü)re,* which may be translated by 'for, to, in order to'. The negation is *ülü.*

abura
idere
oi ayula-yi yaiqara   in order to behold the woods and
     mountain
juljayan-iyan idere   in order to eat her own young

c) **Conditional Gerund.** This form denotes an act which is a necessary condition (logical or temporal) of the following action coming into effect, and has the ending *-basu / -besü* (*-ubasu* etc. after *b* and *r*). It may be translated by a clause in 'if, when' (*cf.* the dual meaning of Ger. *wenn*). The negation is *ese.*

abubasu
idebesü
qola-ača qarbuju alabasu   When they killed it, by shooting
     from afar
teimü busu bolbasu   If it be otherwise (than) so

The modern language uses a form in *-bala / -bele.*

d) **Terminative Gerund.** This form indicates an action, which when finished permits the main action to begin. It ends in *-tala / -tele,* and may be translated by 'while, as soon as, as long as'. The negation is *ülü.*

abtala
idetele
nayur-un jaqa-dur küliyejü   While they stood waiting at the
baitala   edge of the lake
kürtele   going as far as; until

Reading Selection

IV. The Lion and the Hare*

*nigen γajar-a arsalan taulai qoyar qamtu baiγsan-ača, arsalan ber
taulai-dur ürgülji omoylaju doromjilan jobaγaqui-dur taulai qaširan
qorosqu sanaγa töröǰü yabuγsan-ača¹ nigen yeke usutu gün quduγ-i
üjeged arsalan-dur ögülerün: 'abaγai a, tanu yaγun kemegsen bükün-i
5 bi küliyekü bolbaču², ende nigen amitan ber "üneger küčütei bolbasu
nada-luγa temečigtün³, teimü busu bolbasu minu boγol bui" kemeǰü
bainam' kemegsen-dür, arsalan omoy ‖ anu badaraju 'qamiγa bainam?
tegün-i nadur üjegül' kemegsen-dür taulai ber quduγ-un dergede abačiγad
'egün-ü dotora baina' kemegsen-e arsalan önggüiǰü üjeged, niγur-iyan
10 aturiγulqu ba soyoγa-ban irjailyaqu terigüten-i üiledkü-dür, usun-u
dotora ču mön teimü dürsü γaruγsan-i amitan bolγan sanaju quduγ-un
dotora qaraiγad ükügsen-iyer, taulai ber noyalaγči ügei bolǰu amurčiluya.*

Vocabulary 6

a vocative particle
abači- to lead, conduct away
abaγai master (address to superior), sire
amitan being, creature, sentient
amurči- to live in peace and quiet
aryamǰi rope
aturiγul- to wrinkle (trans.)
ba and
badara- to flame up
boγol slave
bögesü if there be
busu other, otherwise; not (postp.)
bükün everything
deile- to surpass, conquer
doromjila- to humiliate, insult
dotor interior, inner
  dotor-a in, inside
dürsü form, shape
ese no, not
gün deep
γaiqa- to regard with wonder
γar- to go out; to assume, take on
irjailya- to bare teeth (at one another)

jarliγ decree, order, edict
  jarliγ bol- to command, proclaim; of a royal figure, to say, speak
jobaγa- to torment
juljaγa(n) young, offspring
kilinča sin, fault
küčü(n) strength
  küčütei strong
küliye- to wait; to endure
mordo- to ride off, depart
mön deictic particle, just that one
niγur face
nigültü sinful
noyalaγči tyrant
omoy pride, arrogance
  omoyla- to be proud
ögülel word, statement
önggüi- to crane one's neck
qarai- to spring, leap
qašira- to be bothered
qoros- to become angry
sanaγa thought, memory
soyoγa eyeteeth

---

* *Subhāṣita* 2, fol. 40 r.

¹ *yabuγsan-ača*, freely, 'because he had got into an angry frame of mind'.
² *bükün-i bi küliyekü bolbacu*, 'although I am one who has endured everything'.
³ *nada-luγa temečigtün*, 'let him contend with me'.

tamu hell
temeči- to contend, quarrel
terigü(n) head, beginning
  terigüten those things at the beginning, the rest, *et cetera*
törö- to be born, to arise

ügegüye not
üiled- to do, perform
üjegül- to cause to see, to show
üneger indeed, truthfully
ürgülji incessant
yabu- to travel, wander, go

Lesson Seven

Contents. Personal pronouns; reflexive pronouns; demonstrative pronouns; interrogative and indefinite pronouns; remaining verbal nouns (in *-day, -ya,* and *-l*); adversative gerund (in *-baču*); causative voice; mediopassive voice. Reading Selection: V. The Throne Robber. NB. Owing to the length of Lesson Seven, two study periods are best devoted to it.

§ 35. **Personal Pronouns.** The Mongolian personal pronouns have the same declensional endings as do regular nouns, the only difference being that there are some slightly different forms in the nominative, genitive and accusative for the 1st p. sg. & pl. and the 2nd p. sg.

Singular

Nom.	*bi* I	*či* you (thou)
Gen.	*minu*	*činu*
Acc.	*nama-yi*	*čima-yi*
Dat.-Loc.	*nadur*	*čimadur*
Ablat.	*nadača*	*čimača*
Instr.	*nada-bar*	*čima-bar*
Comit.	*nada-luya*	*čima-luya*

Plural

Nom.	*ba* we	*ta* you
Gen.	*manu*	*tanu*
Acc.	*mani*	*tani*
Dat.-Loc.	*mandur*	*tandur*
Ablat.	*manača*	*tanača*
Instr.	*maniyar*	*taniyar*
Comit.	*manluya*	*tanluya*

The plural of "I" is exclusive (*i.e.*, does not include the person addressed), because it originally meant 'I and the ones about me'. The inclusive plural (you + I = we) is *bide* (gen. *biden-ü*, etc.).
Verbal forms do not necessarily use accompanying personal pronouns, this information being derived from the context.
The genitives of the personal pronouns, *minu, činu, manu, bidenü* and *tanu*, correspond to the pronominal adjectives 'my, your, our' in English.

  minu boyol   the slave of me, my slave

To express 'mine, yours, ours' etc., the suffix *-qai / -kei*, 'the one pertaining to', is used. It also occurs with some other pronouns.

  činükei   yours, that pertaining to you, "das deinige"

3*

§ 36. Reflexive Pronouns. The reflexive pronoun may be expressed by forms of the word *öber* (*öger*), self. This pronoun may occur with all three persons, and may be the nominative subject of a clause.

Nom.	*öber(-iyen)*
Gen.	*öber-ün*
Acc.	*öber-iyen*
Dat.-Loc.	*öber-tegen*

A circumlocution, *beye minu*, my body, myself, is also used in the first person.

§ 37. Demonstrative Pronouns. The pronoun of the third person is not generally expressed, for which reason these have now largely disappeared. The only forms remaining of **i*, he, are *inu*, and (rarely) *imayi* and *imadur*. From **a*, they, the form *anu* remains.

The demonstratives *ene*, this, and *tere*, that, may serve as substitute for a pronoun of the third person.

Singular

Nom.	*ene* this	*tere*	that
Gen.	*egün-ü*	*tegün-ü*	
Acc.	*egün-i*	*tegün-i*	
Dat.-Loc.	*egün-dür*	*tegün-dür*	
Ablat.	*egün-eče*	*tegün-eče*	
Instr.	*egün-iyer*	*tegün-iyer*	
Comit.	*egün-lüge*	*tegün-lüge*	

Plural

Nom.	*ede* these	*tede*	those
Gen.	*eden-ü*	*teden-ü*	
Acc.	*eden-i*	*teden-i*	
Dat.-Loc.	*eden-dür*	*teden-dür*	
Ablat.	*eden-eče*	*teden-eče*	
Instr.	*eden-iyer*	*teden-iyer*	
Comit.	*eden-lüge*	*teden-lüge*	

The forms *ede* and *tede* have the alternate, more emphatic forms *edeger* and *tedeger* (from *ede* + *ber*, *tede* + *ber*)[1], gen. *edeger-ün*, *tedeger-ün*. The words *eimü* and *teimü*, such, such a, are declined as in the table above (gen. *eimü-yin*, *teimü-yin*).

---

[1] The alternation of *g/b*, which can also be observed elsewhere, is due to a confusion of two originally distinct spirants, which both disappeared at an early stage of the history of the Mongolian language, and which consequently appear in the written language now as *b*, now as *g*.

öber,	*öger*	self
debel,	*degel*	cloak
-bar,	*-gar*	instrumental case

§ 38. **Indefinite and Interrogative Pronouns.**

These pronouns are indefinite in dependent clauses and interrogative in main clauses: *ken irebesü* 'if somebody comes', *ken irelüge* 'Who came?' In case of ambiguity *ba* or *ber* is added to characterize a pronoun as indefinite: *ken ber iremüi* 'Someone is coming'.

ken, pl. *ked*	who
yayun	what
ali	which (out of a limited number)
yambar	what kind
kedün	how many; several
kejiye	when
qamiya	where
ker	how
ker be	if
ali . . . ali	either . . . or

§ 39. **Remaining Verbal Nouns.**

a) The **iterative noun** is a form expressing iterative or repeating action, and may also denote frequentative or customary action. It ends in *-(u)day / -(ü)deg*. It is one of the grammatical forms that grows more frequent in recent MSS. Its negative is *ügei*.

abuday	frequent or habitual taking, he who repeatedly takes
idedeg	frequent or habitual eating, he who repeatedly eats
baiday	ordinary, usual

b) The **continuative noun** denotes an action which is always or continuously done. It ends in *-ya / -ge*, and after *-i*, in *-ya / -ye*.

abuya	he who always takes
idege	he who always eats
sanaya	that which is always thought, a memory
tariya	that which is cultivated, a field

The negative used is *ügei*.

c) **Noun in *-l*.** This form sees action not taken in any particular way. It ends in *-(u)l / -(ü)l*.

abul	a taking
irel	a going
ayul	fright
sanal	thought, memory
töröl	birth
inayši irel ügei	without coming over here

The negative is *ügei*, and the form is often used with the negative.
This form may also take a direct object.

ači-yi sanal ügegüi   having no memory of good deeds

§ 40. **Adversative Gerund.** This form has the meaning 'although, though,
in spite of' and ends in *-baču | -bečü*. It derives from the preterite *-ba(i)*
+ *ču*, an emphatic particle. The negation is *ese*.

    bolbaču   although he is one who
    kemebečü   even though he said

§ 41. **Causative Voice.** The meanings of to cause an action to be performed, to have an action done, to see that someone does an action,
or to leave it to another to perform an action are expressed in Mongolian
by the causative voice of the verb. This is formed with the suffixes
-γa- | -ge- (after *b*, *d* and *s*: *-qa- | -ke-* and after *i*: *-ya- | -ye-*) and *-γul- | -gül-*
(chiefly after vowels). With verb stems in *-γu-* haplology produced forms
like (preclassical) *saγul-* 'to set' from *saγu-* 'to sit', which were then
reinforced by the normal suffix *-γa-*: *saγulγa-*. This suffix *-lγa- | -lge-*
has now been extended to many vowel stems.

    üje-   to see
    üjegül-   to make see, to show
    ide-   to eat
    idegül-   to give to eat, to feed
    saγu-   to sit
    saγulγa-   to seat, to appoint
    bol-   to be, to become
    bolγa-   to cause to be, to make
    buča-   to turn back, return (intr.)
    bučaγa-   to make turn back, return (tr.)
    emüs-   to dress (intr.)
    emüske-   to clothe, dress (tr.)
    bos-   to rise
    bosqa-   to raise
    ǰoki-   to be suitable, fit in
    ǰokiγa-   to compose, create, fashion
    baγu-   to descend, to camp
    baγulγa-   to cause to descend, to settle in a
                                    camp (tr.)

§ 42. **Medio-Passive Voice.** The passive of Western languages is the
mere opposite of the transitive-intransitive dichotomy of the active
voice. The Mongolian medio-passive, however, is not in opposition to
the active voice, but another function of it, and, in that the action
reflects on the subject, middle as well. The passive is, in effect, construed
as a medial causative. The endings are *-γda- | -gde-* after vowels and
-da- | -de- after consonants. After *b*, *d*, *g*, *r* and *s*, the ending is *-ta- | -te-*.

ab-	to take
abta-	to be taken
ide-	to eat
idegül-	to give to eat
idegde-	to give (one's self to someone) to eat, to be eaten
bari-	to seize, take
bariγul-	to cause to take, to hand over
bariγda-	to cause (somebody else) to take (the speaker), to be taken

Agency with the passive is expressed by the dative case.

qaγan bars-tur miqa idegülbei	The king let the tiger eat meat
qaγan bars-tur idegdebei	The king let the tiger eat him: the king was eaten by the tiger

Reading Selection

V. The Throne Robber*

dumda oron-u nigen qaγan ber Ruto neretü nigen ǰiγasuči kümün-i
tüšimel bolγan debšigülügsen-iyer tere maγu kümün küčütü boluγad
ači-yi sanal ügegüi qaγan-i qoroγan, qaγan-u köbegün Dharma-bala
kiged Bala neretü qoγar-i kögeǰü orkiγad, öber-iyen qaγan-u širegen-e
5 *saγuǰu, uridaki qaγan-u tüšimel Šinti-bikrahi neretü-dür ῾čima-yi buu*
alasuγai¹, minu tüšimel bol²᾽ kemegsen-e tere tüšimel ese bolǰuqui.
tegün-e tere tüšimel-i bariǰu nigen gün quduγ-un dotora oroγuluγad
edür-ün niǰeged³ emkü γulir ba nigen uγuči ‖ usun-iγar ǰilmegülǰü
γurban sara boluγsan-u qoina γarγaǰu irebesü mašida ečiged šira üsün
10 *inu segseiǰü tamir γekede doroidaγsan aǰuγu⁴. tegün-e ῾edüge minu*
tüšimel bol᾽ kemebečü ese boluγsan-dur, tere maγu qaγan ögülerün ῾ene
sain uqaγatai tula alabasu qairan bainam⁵; daisun tula egün-i saγulγaǰu
ülü bolqu; kiǰaγar-tur čüleǰü kögegtün⁶᾽ kemeǰü kögelgebei.
tendeče tere tüšimel ber uridaki qaγan-u qoγar köbegün-i erigseger
15 *γabuǰu, nigen γaǰar-a olan keüked dotora baiqu-yi oluγad teǰiγeǰü*
üčügen ösügsen⁷ čaγ-tur nigen širege ǰasaǰu Dharma-bala-yi saγulγaγad,
tüšimel öber-iyen ölǰei orošiγulqu terigüten sain beleg ǰokiγabai⁸.

---

* *Subhāṣita* 2, fol. 26 v., ff.

¹ *čima-yi buu alasuγai*, lit., don't let me have to kill you, *i.e.*, I shall not kill you.
² *bol*, the pure stem serves as imperative of the 2nd p. sg., 'be, become'.
³ *edür-ün niǰeged*, 'once a day'.
⁴ *aǰuγu*, translate 'being, was (were)'.
⁵ *qairan bainam*, 'that would be a pity'.
⁶ *kögegtün*, 'drive him away'.
⁷ *üčügen ösügsen*, 'grown to young manhood'.
⁸ *terigüten sain beleg ǰokiγabai*, 'he bestowed all manner of good gifts and similar things'.

tegüneče ulam-iyar albatu ulus-i baya saya olǰu čögeken čerig beledüged, tedegerün unulya-dur imayta eme ǰayan-i čuylayulǰu baǰayabai.
20 *tegüneče ǰiyasuči qayan-dur čeriglejü oduysan-dur tere qayan olan čerig abču mordoǰu ireged, ‖ olan yeke ǰayan-nuyud-i talbiqui-dur inadu Dharmabala-yin čerig ber eme ǰayan-nuyud-i uytuyulǰu talbibai. tedeger yeke ǰayan-nuyud ber eme ǰayan-nuyud-i üǰeged inayši irel ügei gedergü bučaǰu öber-ün čerig-iyen tobray bolyaqui-luya qamtuda Dharmabala-yin*
25 *čerig ber[9] ǰiyasuči-yin čerig-i kögeged mašida doroidayulǰu törö-yi inu buliyayad Dharma-bala-yi širegen-e sayulyaǰu qayan bolyaluya.*

Vocabulary 7

ači good deed, benefaction
albatu subject, inferior
ali which (of several), where, what
ba and; we
baya saya little by little
baiday usual, ordinary
baǰaya- to prepare, arrange
beled- to prepare, set up
beleg gift, present
beye body, self
bide we (inclusive)
buliya- to take possession of
buča- to turn back
buu prohibitive particle
čerig soldier; army; war
čerigle- to wage war
či thou, you
čima- oblique stem of *či*
čögeken some few
čuylayul- to collect, assemble
čüle- to banish
daisun enemy
debšigül- to appoint; promote
doroida- to be weakened
doroidayul- to vanquish
dumda middle, center
  dumda oron middle land, i. e., India; China
eče- to grow thin, emaciate
edüge now
edür day

egün- oblique stem of *ene*
emkü mouthful, morsel, bit
eri- to seek, request
gedergü back, backwards
yarya- to take out, bring out
yulir meal, ground grain
idegde- to be eaten
idegül- to feed, give to eat
imayta exclusive, sole
inadu existing, on this side
inayši hither, to this side
ǰayan elephant (pl. *-nuyud*)
ǰasa- to set up, fix
ǰiyasu(n) fish
ǰiyasuči fisherman
ǰilmegül- to punish
ǰokiya- to make, fashion
  beleg ǰokiya- to give gifts
keǰiye once, when
ker how
keüken child (pl. *-d*)
ki- to make, construct
kiged and
kiǰayar border, edge, shore
köge- to turn out, hunt down
kögelge- to have driven away
mayu bad, evil, poor
manu- oblique stem of *ba*
mašida very, extremely
minu- oblique stem of *bi*
mordo- to set out, travel
nadur, namayi see *bi*

---

[9] *inayši irel ügei* ..., 'Without coming over here (to our battle lines), they turned back, and what with (the elephants) having trampled their own soldiers into the dust, the army of Dharma-bala routed ...'.

nijeged one at a time
orki- to cast, break, loose (perfectivizing auxiliary)
oroγul- to place in, have enter
oron place; opportunity
orošiγul- to establish, bring about, introduce
öber-iyen oneself
öljei fortune, happiness
ös- to grow up
qaira(n) love, sympathy, pity
qamtuda with, together with (postpositional), simultaneous
qoina after, since (postp.)
qoroγa- to kill
sayulγa- to seat, appoint
sanal remembrance, memory, thought
sara(n) moon, month
segsei- to be dishevelled
šira yellow

širege(n) table, throne
talbi- to put, place, arrange
tamir power, force
tanu- oblique stem of *ta*
tegün-e in this = then
tejiye- to rear, bring up
tende-eče from there, thereupon
tobray dust, ground
törö kingdom, law
töröl birth
uytuyul- to meet, send to meet
uyuči swallow, gulp
unulya riding animal
uqaya(n) reason, intellect
uqayatai intelligent
ügegüi not existing
üjegül- to show
ülü no, not
üsün hair
yambar which, what sort
yekede greatly to a high degree

Lesson Eight

Contents. Reciprocal voice; particles (negative, interrogative, prohibitive, vocative); postpositions; numerals (cardinal, ordinal, collective). Reading Selection: VI. The Hungry Tigress (Part One).

§ 43. Reciprocal Voice. The reciprocal voice denotes action performed by several persons in cooperation, either working against one another or for each other. Its suffixes are *-ldu-*/*-ldü-* and *-lča-*/*-lče-*.

keme-	to say
kemeldü-	to say as with one voice
asayu-	to ask
asayulča-	to ask each other

There is however a distinct tendency to use *-ldu-* about reciprocal relations and *-lča-* about joint actions:

bari-	to take, to seize
barildu-	to seize each other, to wrestle
ide-	to eat
idelče-	to eat something together
yabu-	to wander, to travel
yabulča-	to journey together (as a family)
alaldu-	to fight one another (not a common enemy)
qudaldu-	to trade, to buy and sell

§ 44. Particles.

a) **Negative.** Negation is expressed in Mongolian by the use of the particles *ese, ülü,* which occur before the verb, or by the nouns *busu, ügei,* which occur after a noun or verbal noun.

ese bolǰuqui	he did not become
ese abubai.	He did not buy it.
irekü ügei.	He will not come.

Both particles occur with all non-nominal finite forms except the imperatives etc. The particle *ese* must be used with certain gerunds and verbal nouns and *ülü* with other forms. *ügei* has the meaning of 'non-existence'. *busu* really means 'other, different' and still retains that meaning when it precedes the element modified.

busu morin	another horse
morin busu	different from a horse.
morin ügei	without a horse

b) The **prohibitive particle** is *buu,* do not. It serves to negate imperatives.

čima-yi buu alasuyai.	Don't let me have to kill you; I shall not kill you.

c) The **interrogative particle** is *u* or *uu* (after a vowel, *yu*).

yeke qaɣan-u ene mön u?	Is this here the great king's?

d) **Vocative particles.** In addressing or calling to a person (especially of higher position), the particles *ai* and *a* are often used. *ai* occurs before the noun, and *a* after it.

ai qoyar aqa minu	Oh, my two elder brothers!
abaɣai a	Oh, master!

§ 45. **Postpositions.** Prepositions as such are unknown in Mongolian. Instead, the language possesses a number of postpositions, mostly of nominal origin, which occur after the word with which they form a phrase.

qudalduɣči-luɣa qamtu	together with a merchant
tere metü	like this, in this manner
ene sain tula	because he (is) good
ɣurban sara qoina	after three months
minu tula	on account of me

The negative *ügei* occurs in a postposed position. Some other words also occur after the nouns with which they are associated in meaning, and are mostly in the dative-locative case.

noyalaɣči ügei	without a tyrant
kereg ügei	without cause, there is no reason
minu morin ügei-yin tula	because I have no horse
bars-un emüne	in front of the tiger
oi-yin dotor-a	in the forest
deger-e	above, over

§ 46. Numerals.

a) The **cardinal** numerals are as follows.

1.	*nigen*	10.	*arban*
2.	*qoyar*	20.	*qorin*
3.	*yurban*	30.	*yučin*
4.	*dörben*	40.	*döčin*
5.	*tabun*	50.	*tabin*
6.	*jiryuyan*	60.	*jiran*
7.	*doloyan*	70.	*dalan*
8.	*naiman*	80.	*nayan*
9.	*yisün*	90.	*yeren*

100.	*jayun*
1,000.	*mingyan*
10,000.	*tümen*

b) The **ordinal** numerals are formed with the suffix *-duyar / -düger*, e.g., *naimaduyar*, eighth. The word *terigün*, 'head, beginning' also occurs in the meaning of 'first', as does *angqaduyar* (from *angqan*, 'beginning'). The word *kedün*, 'how many', has a form *kedüdüger*, 'what number, how many?'. A few numbers have slightly irregular forms in the ordinal series.

qoyaduyar	second
yutayar	third
dötöger	fourth
tabtayar, tabudayar	fifth

c) **Collective** numerals, meaning 'a group of two, three' *etc.*, may be formed with the suffix *-yula / -güle*.

qoyayula	the two of them
yurbayula	the three of them
dörbegüle	the four of them
olayula	many at a time

To express 'so many at a time' the ending *-yad / -ged* is used, *i.e.*, *nijeged*, one at a time, *yurbayad*, three at a time. They are plurals in *-d*, starting from *jiryuyad* and *doloyad*, which latter forms have then influenced the rest of the numerals. To express the number of times, the suffix *-ta / -te* is used: *nigente*, once, *qoyarta*, twice, *yurbanta*, thrice, etc.

Reading Selection

VI. The Hungry Tigress (Part One)

The text is transcribed after I. J. Schmidt, *Grammatik der mongolischen Sprache*, St. Petersburg, 1831, pp. 131—134. Some variant readings are added from the xylograph in the Copenhagen collection of the *üliger-ün dalai*, fol. 13v1 to 15v9 (Peking, 1714).
Words in parentheses occur in the Schmidt text, but not in the xylograph, and words in brackets occur in the xylograph but not in Schmidt's

text. The sign / divides the variant readings, first Schmidt, then the xylograph. Quotation marks and punctuation have been added for sake of clarity.

If the student desires to begin the reading of Mongolian script now, let him turn directly to the section in this book on the Mongolian script. After study of this section, he may then begin the story in the native script, using the transcription below as a guide and check. To aid in ready reference, the sign ‖ denotes the division of lines in the script section.

erte toya tomši ügei¹ nögčigsen galab-un urida anu, ene čambudvib-tur Yeke Terge² neretü qayan bülüge. tere qayan-dur qariya-‖-tu mingyan toyatan (üčügüken / üčügen) qad buyu, yurban köbegün buyu; yeke köbegün anu Maha-Nada neretü buyu, dumdatu köbegün anu Maha-‖
5 -Diba nere-tü buyu, odqan köbegün anu Maha-Saduva neretü (bolai / buyu). tere odqan köbegün anu ücügen-eče asaraqui nigülesküi ‖ sedkiltü boluyad, qamuy bügüde-yi yayča köbegün-dür adali sedkimüi³.
tere čay-tur tere qayan anu noyad tüšimed qatud ‖ selte-ber oi ayula-yi yaiqara üjen oduyad sayun büküi-dür, yurban köbegün ber oi-yin
10 dotora yaiqara oduysan-dur, ‖ nigen bars ǰuljayalaju maši ölösün umdayasču ǰuljayan-iyan idere kürküi⁴ üjejü, tedüi odqan köbegün anu qoyar aqa-‖ -nar-tur-iyan ögülerün: 'ai qoyar aqa minu, ene ölögčin bars anu öl ügei boluysan-iyar ǰuljayan-iyan idemüi', kemen ‖ ögülegsen--dür, qoyar aqa (inu / anu) ögülerün 'ene bars maši ölösügsen-iyer
15 mayad ǰuljayan-iyan idemüi-ja', kemen ögülegsen-‖ -dür, basa odqan köbegün anu qoyar aqa-dayan ögülerün 'ene bars-un ideši yayun (bui kemen)' asayuysan-dur, qoyar aqa-‖ -nar anu ögülerün, 'aliba šine alaysan noitan miqa čisun bögesü⁵, bars-un ideši buyu-ja', kemen ögülegsen-dür, basa odqan ‖ köbegün ögülerün, 'ken ber öber-ün miqa
20 čisun-iyar egün-ü amin-i aburan čidamui?'⁶ kemen asayuysan-dur, qoyar aqa anu ögüler-‖ -ün 'teimü maši berke üiles-iyer egün-ü amin-i (aburaqui / aburaysan) ken čidamui?' kemen ögülebesü, tedüi odqan köbegün inu ein kemen sedkimüi, ‖ 'bi öni orčilang-dur orčiju'⁷, amin beyeben toya tomši ügei qoor qomsa bolyaluya⁸ ; ǰarim-dur inu tačiyangyui

---

¹ toya tomši ügei, 'amount without number', i.e., countless. The entire phrase reads 'Once upon a time, countless past ages ago . . .'.
² 'yeke terge' renders the Sanskrit name Mahā-ratha. The other names in the next sentence are Mahā-nada, Mahā-deva and Mahā-sattva.
³ qamuy . . . sedkimüi, 'considered everything and everyone like (he would) an only son'.
⁴ idere kürküi, 'on the point of eating'.
⁵ bögesü, 'what there may be', i.e., any.
⁶ ken ber . . . čidamui? 'Can anyone . . .?'
⁷ bi öni . . . orčiju. 'I, turning in long turnings', refers to the Buddhistic concept of the wheel of life. Translate 'I have been revolving on the wheel of life for a long time'.
⁸ amin . . . bolyaluya, 'I have performed countless evils of the living body.'

25 *-yin tula,* ‖ *ǰarim-dur anu urin(-u) tula, ǰarim-dur anu mungqaγ-un*
tulada, qabiya tusa ügei bolγaγsan buyu-ǰa [9]. *nom-un tulada öglige* ‖ *ögkü*
oron-luγa [ese] učiraǰu bülüge [10]. *edüge qabiya tusa bolγaqu-yin tulada*
beyeben egün-dür ögsügei' [11] *kemen sedkiǰü bürün,* ‖ *tedüi γurbaγula*
qariǰu ireküi ǰaγura, odqan köbegün anu qoγar aqa-daγan ein kemen
30 *ögülerün, 'ta qoγaγula uridqan-a* ‖ *yabutuγai* [12]'.

Vocabulary 8*

abura- to save, rescue
ai vocative particle, Oh!
alaldu- to kill, fight one another
ali-ba every, any
ami(n) life, spirit, soul
angqa(n) beginning
asara- to commiserate, sympathize
barildu- to wrestle
berke hard, strong, difficult
bolai = buyu
čambudvib world, Indian continent
čida- to be able; can
dalai sea
degere above, over
ein such, so, in this manner
emüne in front of
erte once, once upon a time
galab eon, age
γayča only, sole, alone
γaiqa- to behold, admire, consider
    with wonder
idelče- to eat together
ideši food, meals
ǰaγura while, during
ǰarim some
ǰulǰaγala- to give birth to
    ǰulǰaγan young, offspring
mayad certain(ly)
mingγan thousand

mön deictic particle, just that one
mungqaγ ignorance   [there
nigüles- to commiserate, be merci-
    ful, sympathize
niǰeged one at a time
noitan fresh, moist
nom belief, doctrine, religion,
nögči- to pass (of time)   [dharma
orči- to turn
orčilang revolution, rebirth cycle
öglige alms, charity
öl food
ölögčin female animal
ölös- to be hungry
öni long
qabiya benefit, use, profit
qamuγ all, everything
qari- to return
qariya subject
    qariyatu subordinate, vassal
qomsa little, lowly
qoor evil, deceit
qoor qomsa harm, damage
sedki- to think
    sedkil thought
    sedkiltü disposed
selte party, company; together with
šine new
tačiya- to desire, love

---

[9] *qabiya tusa* ... *buyu-ǰa,* 'have indeed become (persons) without profit
or use'.
[10] *ögkü* ... *bülüge,* 'I have met with (no) opportunity to give ...'.
[11] *ögsügei,* 'let me give, I am going to give'.
[12] *yabutuγai,* imperative, 'do (you two) go on (a little ahead)'.

* To conserve space, the cardinal and other numbers in the lesson text
  are not entered in the vocabulary, but will all be found in the Glossary.

tačiyangyu desire, love, lust
tedüi immediately, thereupon
terge wagon, chariot
toya number, amount
  toyatan numbered
tomši (now obsolete), number
  tomši ügei countless
tula, tulada postp., on account of,
  in order to, for the sake of

tusa usefulness, utility
umdayas- to be thirsty
uridqan a little ahead, in front of
urin anger
üčügen little, small; youth, young
  üčügüken minor, subordinate
üile deed, action, matter
üliger story, tale
yabulča- to journey together

Lesson Nine

Contents. Imperatives; use of the accusative; the verb 'to be'; adverbs & conjunctions. Reading Selection: VI. The Hungry Tigress (Part Two).

§ 47. **Imperatives.**

a) The **normal imperative** of the 2nd p. is expressed by the pure stem.

ab	take
ide	eat
minu tüšimel bol.	Be my minister!

The polite form has the ending *-(u)ytun / -(ü)gtün* (archaic *-dqun / -dkün*).

abuytun	take
idegtün	eat
kögegtün	Drive (him) away!

b) The **intentional imperative** is used in the 1st and 2nd persons, and ends in *-suyai / -sügei* (archaic texts have *-su / -sü*).

absuyai	I am going to take, let me take
idesügei	I am going to eat, let me eat
ögsügei	I am going to give, let me give.

c) The **voluntative imperative**, which may have cohortative overtones, is used in the 1st and 3rd persons, and ends in *-(u)ya / -(ü)ye.*

abuya	let me (him) take
ideye	let me (him) eat.

d) The **optative imperative** expresses the desire that something may happen, and occurs in the 2nd and 3rd persons. It ends in *-tuyai / -tügei.*

abtuyai	grant that he may take
idetügei	grant that he may eat
uridqan-a yabutuyai.	Go on to a spot ahead.

An archaic form in *-yasai / -gesei* may also be met.

e) The **timetive imperative** expresses apprehension. It ends in *-(u)γujai /
-(ü)güjei*.

abuγujai	What if he takes
idegüjei	What if he eats.

f) The **passive imperative**. An imperative of impersonal nature may
be expressed by a form in *-(u)γdaqu(i) / -(ü)gdekü(i)*, originally the
passive infinitive. It is best translated by an ordinary imperative,
rather than by a 'there shall be . . .' phrase.

abuγdaqui	Please take! (replaces *abtaqui*)
idegdekü i	Please eat!
ta ülü jobaγdaqu.	Do not grieve (lit. there shall not be grieving, or 'it is not to be grieved')
tegün-i bariγdaqui	Seize it!

§ 48. **Use of the Accusative.** At the beginning of a sentence or clause,
an accusative may be used to indicate that the word is not subject to
the final verb but to the closest verb.

čima-yi kürüged sača tedeger	As soon as you have come, they
bügüde bosču iremüi.	will all rise and come (at you).

If instead of *čima-yi*, the nominative *či* were used, the meaning would
be reversed, as *či . . . iremüi* can only mean 'you come (at them)'.

nama-yi ireküi čaγ-tur	at the time of my coming

A use of *bi* would be understood to refer to some verb yet to come.

§ 49. **The Verb 'To Be'.** The verb 'to be' in Mongolian, as in many
other languages, displays a variety of stems. Their use can be delineated
as follows.

a) The stem *a-* occurs in the durative form *amui*, he is; the gerund of
absolute subordination *an*, being; the gerund of purpose *ara*, in order
to be; the coordinative gerund *aγad*, the terminative gerund *atala*,
and the preterite participle *aγsan*. The form *ajuγu* is distinctly *sui
generis*, but may be said to correspond to a form in *-juqui*.

The original and only stem is *bü-* but from the effect of the vowels *e* in
following syllables, a secondary form *bö-* has developed, and some prefer
to transcribe it that way.

b) The stem *bö- / bü-*. The stem *bü-* occurs in *bülüge*, he has been,
bükü(i), to be, and *bürün*, being, forms in which an *ü* occurs in the
second syllable, while the stem *bö-* occurs only in the forms *böged*,
bögesu and *bögetele*.

c) The stem *bai-* has developed from its original meaning of 'to stand,
wait, remain, dwell' into a synonym of 'to be'. It first becomes common
after 1700. In the durative tense, it has the form *bainam* (modern
baina), he is.

d) The stem *bol-*, 'to become' is also used for 'to be', especially in such forms as *bolbai*, he was, *bolai*, *bolumui*, he is, *bolun*, being, and *bolbaču*, even though it be, however. The stem *bol-* is further used in compounds, as —*ju bol-*, to be able (see § 54).

e) The noun *bui*, or *buyu*, the being, is the equivalent of Turkish *var*, 'what is, there is, there are'. The opposite meaning is furnished by *ügei* (Turkish *yok*).

bars bui.	There are (things called) tigers; tigers exist (es gibt Tiger).
bars ügei.	There are no tigers.

When the interrogative particle *u* is added, *bui* becomes *buyu*, and thus coincides with the emphatic form *buyu*.

f) The verb 'to be' in the present tense is however generally omitted.

ene sain	That is good.
maha-saduva qamiya?	Where is Mahā-sattva?
ta ayuqu kereg ügei.	There is no cause for you to fear.

But note:

ene bülüge.	That was it.

§ 50. **Adverbs and Conjunctions.** Many adverbs and conjunctions are in actuality forms of nouns or verbs.

kiged	and
buyu	or
qamiy-a	where? (dat.-loc.)
üneger	indeed (instr. of *ünen*, truth)
ende	here
tende	there
endeče	from here, hence
tendeče	from there, thence, thereupon, next
egün-e	there, to there
tegün-e	in that, then, thereupon
tegünče	from it, after that

Other adverbs of place, time, manner, *etc.*, will not be listed here, as their meanings are readily ascertained from the glossary.

Reading Selection
VI. The Hungry Tigress (Part Two)

'*bi öber-ün nigen üile-yin tula oi-dur oduyad, kereg-iyen bütügejü ödter-e iresügei*[1] *kemen ögüleged, tere* ‖ *mör-iyer ölögčin bars qamiya bükü tere jüg-tür kürüged, bars-un emüne kebtegsen-dür, bars aman-iyan jayuraju iden ese* ‖ *čidabai. tedüi qan köbegün anu (nigen) quyurqai*
5 *modun-iyar beye-ben qadquju čisun yaryaysan-dur, bars ber čisun-i [inu] doliyayad* ‖ *aman-iyan negen čidayad, beye-deki miqan inu*

---

[1] *iresügei*, I shall come.

baratala idebei². *öni udaysan-dur qoyar aqa-nar inu, 'degü biden-ü* ‖
udabai. yayun-u šiltayan bolbai?' kemen sedkiged, mön kü tere mör-iyer
erin odtala³ ein sedkir-ün 'degü manu mayad beye-ben ‖ *ölösügsen*
10 *bars-tur ögkü-yin tula oduysan buyu-ja', kemen sedkijü tere bars-un*
dergede kürügsen-dür, köbegün-i bars idejü, ‖ *yasun inu čaiju büküi*
üjeged, beyeben köser-e deleddün üküdkübei. egüri boluyad amiduraju
yeke dayun-iyar ukilan köser-e ‖ *körben basa kü üküdkübei.*

tere čay-tur eke qatun inu ein jegüdülerün, yurban kegürjigen-e anu
15 *qotala nayadču nisün yabutala,* ‖ *nigen üčügen-i inu qarčayai bariysan-i*
jegüdüleged sača, serigsen-dür maši ayun emiyeged qayan-dur öčirün
'ai yeke qayan, ‖ *qayučin üge-dür "kegürjigene šibayun köbegün-ü*
sünesün bui⁴", kemen sonosuluya; bi qorumqan udaysan-dur jegüdün-dür
minu, ‖ *yurban kegürjigene nayadču yabun atala, nigen üčügen ke-*
20 *gürjigene-yi qarčayai abču oduysan-i jegüdülebei, mayad odqan kö-*
begün ‖ *minu mayu bolbai ja', kemen ögüleged sača, qamuy bügüde-yi*
erire ilegegsen-dür inu, qorum nigen boluysan-dur qoyar aqa ‖ *inu*
ireged, odqan inu ese iregsen-dür, 'maha-saduva ali?' kemen asayuysan-
-dur, qoyar aqa inu yayun ber ögülen yadaju ‖ *qorum ayad 'bars-tur*
25 *idegdebei' kemen ögülebesü, tedüi qatun eke anu teimü mayu üges-i*
sonosuyad sača köser-e unan ‖ *üküdkübei. qorum nigen boluyad delürejü*
(busu / bosču) qamuy nököd selte bügüdeger köbegün-ü nirvan boluysan
tere oron-dur⁵ odbasu, ‖ *bars inu köbegün-ü miqa-yi čöm idejü, čisun*
inu yajar-tur dusuju yasun čaiju büku-yi üjeged, tedüi qatun eke
30 *terigün-* ‖ *-eče anu bariyad, qayan anu yar-ača bariju yeke (dayun-*
-iyar / dayubar) okilayad üküdkün unabai. qorumqan qarin bosbai.

Vocabulary 9

ama(n) mouth
amidura- to come to oneself
bara- to conclude, make an end of
basa kü again
boluyujai perhaps
bos- to arise, stand up
buyu or
bütüge- to conclude, complete
čai- to bleach, turn white
čöm complete
deled- to strike, beat
delüre- to come to oneself
doliya- to lick

dusu- to flow, drip
egüri long
emiye- to become frightened
emüne before, in front of
ende here
endeče hence, from here
ilege- to send, dispatch
jayura- to close together
jegüdüle- to dream
jegüdün a dream
kebte- to lie
kegürjigene dove, pigeon
körbe- to roll on the ground

² *beye-deki miqan inu baratala idebei*, ate up (ate to completion) the flesh
in his body.
³ *erin odtala*, while they were going seeking.
⁴ *kegürjigene šibayun köbegün-ü sünesün bui*, a dove bird is the symbolic
representation of a son.
⁵ *köbegün-ü nirvan boluysan tere oron-dur*, to the place where the boy
attained Nirvana.

4 Grønbech

kü reinforcing particle
köser earth
mayu bol- to be injured, get hurt
mön reinforcing particle
   mön kü just that one
mör way, road
   tere mör-iyer along that road
nayad- to play
nege- to open
nirvan Nirvana
nis- to fly
nökör friend, comrade
okila- to complain, bemoan, lament
öči- to tell, say (to superior)
ödter quickly
qadqu- to stick, stab
qayučin old, ancient
   qayučin üge proverb

qarčayai falcon, hawk
qorum(qan) moment, while
qotola, all, every
quyurqai torn off piece
sača at once, immediately
seri- to awake
sünesün soul, life's breath, essence
   of personality
šibayun bird
šiltayan cause, reason
tende there
   tendeče thence, from there
uda- to pass (of time); to delay,
   stay away
üge word, saying
üküdkü- to faint
yada- to be unable.
yasu(n) bone

Lesson Ten

Contents. Strengthening suffixes; word formation in nouns; word formation in verbs; compound verbs; nominal suffixes. Reading Selection: VI. The Hungry Tigress (Part Three).

§ 51. **Strengthening Suffixes.** The particles *kü* and *ču* serve to emphasize the previous word. The particle *ja* occurs mostly with verbs, and may be translated 'indeed, to be sure, certainly', *etc.* Of like function is *-a.*

    mön kü   just that one there, namely
    buyu-ja, bui-ja   he is indeed, he certainly is
    amui-a   it is indeed

§ 52. **Word Formation in Nouns.**

a) The **nomen actoris** in *-či* denotes the person performing the action logically associated with the noun from which it is derived. The plural is in *-d.*

    qoni(n)   sheep
    qoniči   shepherd
    jiyasu(n)   fish
    jiyasuči   fisherman
    modu(n)   tree, wood
    moduči   woodworker, carpenter

b) The derivative suffix in *-tu / -tü* or *-tai / -tei* (the latter originally a feminine form), plural *-tan / -ten*, denotes the person having or possessed of the object denoted by the noun.

qonitu	sheepowner, one having sheep
moritu	owning a horse, a rider
amitan	living creature(s)
küčün	strength
küčütei	strong
arya	craft, wile
aryatu	cunning, sly
činggis nere	the name Gengis
činggis neretü	having the name Gengis, called Gengis

c) *-daki / -deki* (locative in *-da*, § 14, and *-ki*), after vowels, *l, m, n,* and *-taki / -teki* otherwise, denotes the one who is in (a thing).

köbege-deki	the one on the shore
usun-u köbege-deki modun	the tree at the water's edge
uridaki	the one in the beginning, the original
beye-deki miqan	the flesh in his body
yajar-takin-dur	to those on earth

d) The addition of *-qan / -ken* to a word strengthens the quality in that word.

oira	near
oiraqan	very near
sain	good
saiqan	pretty good, beautiful
ene	this
eneken	this one
üčügen	small, young
üčügüken	minor, subordinate
urida	before, previous
uridqan	a little before
nigeken	only one
qoyarqan	only two

§ 53. **Word Formation in Verbs.** The most frequent suffixes which may form verbs from nouns and adjectives are *-la / -le, -ra / -re, -da / -de,* and *-šiya / -šiye.* These verbs may of course have their own derivative forms, as the passive and reciprocal.

4 *

čerig	soldier; army
čerigle-	to wage war
morin	horse
morila-	to ride, travel
omoy	pride
omoyla-	to be proud
köke	blue
kökere-	to become blue
doroi	weakness
doroida-	to be weak
doroidayul-	to weaken (tr.)
yekede-	to become large
bayada-	to become small
sain	good
saišiya-	to approve, recommend
ǰöb	excellent, fine
ǰöbšiye-	to approve, recognize as worthy

§ 54. **Compound Verbs.** Two juxtaposed verbs often describe one action, each of the two verbs helping to determine the other.

abču ire-	to take and come = to bring
ǰiyan od-	to go showing = to inform
qariǰu ire-	to return, (intrans.)
kürčü ire-	to arrive

The **potential** verb is expressed by a compound with *čida-*, to be able.

iden čida-	to be able to eat
negen čida-	to be able to open
aburan čida-	to be able to save

A compound with *ög-*, 'to give', imparts the meaning of 'in favor of or on behalf of someone else'.

eriǰü ög-	to seek on behalf of

The use of *yar-* and *oro-* conveys the meanings of 'in' and 'out'.

nisčü yarbai.	He flew out.
nisčü orobai.	He flew in.

Another way of expressing 'to be able' is to use the verb *bol-* with a preceding form in *-ǰu*.

ǰoyoylaǰu bolqu	to be able to consume
yabuǰu bolqu	to be able to go

§ 55. **Nominal suffixes.** Some of the more frequent suffixes which will be found on nouns are the following.

a) *-sun / -sün.*

balyasun	city
negüresün	charcoal

b) *-lang / -leng.*

bayasqulang	happiness, rejoicing
üküleng	death

c) *-ši.*
   ide-   to eat
   ideši   food
d) *-liγ | -lig.*
   bayaliγ   riches
   čečiglig   garden, park
e) *-dal | -del.*
   yabudal   conduct
   üküdel   body, corpse
f) *-γan | -gen.*
   qubilγan   reincarnation
   idegen   food

Reading Selection

VI. The Hungry Tigress (Part Three)

*tere Maha-‖ -Saduva köbegün anu tende-eče üküged sača, tegüs bayasqu-
lang-un oron-dur tngri-yin köbegün bolun töröbei. tere tngri-yin köbegün ‖
anu 'bi yambar sain üile üiledügsen-iyer ende töröbei?', kemen sedkiged,
tngris-ün nidüber tabun jayayan-dur šinjilen¹ ‖ üjebesü, öber-ün*
5 *ükügsen yasun anu nigen oi-yin dotora ečige eke terigülen qamuγ
nököd-iyer küriyelegüljü yeke ‖ dayun-iyar enelün yasalqu-yi [anu]
üjeged, tere tngri-yin köbegün anu ein sedkirün, 'manu tere ečige eke
qoyar anu minu tula maši ‖ yeke jobabasu, beye nasun-dur todqur
bolumui-ja; teden-ü sedkil-i sergügekü-yin tulada odsuyai bi' kemen*
10 *sedkijü, tedüi ‖ [oytaryui-bar ireged degere] oytaryui-dur baiju², eldeb
jüil sain üges-iyer ečige eke qoyar-un sedkil-i sergügebei. ečige eke
qoyar anu oytaryui-‖-dur degegši üjeged 'ai tngri, či ken bui? mandur
jarliγ boluγdaqui³' kemen ögülegsen-dür, tere tngri-yin köbegün ögülerün,
'bi ‖ tanu köbegün Maha-Saduva neretü bui-ja. bi öber-ün beyeben*
15 *ölögčin bars-tur öggügsen-ü ači-bar, tegüs bayasqulang-‖-tu oron-daki
tngri-yin köbegün bolun töröbei. ai qayan ečige qatun eke minu ta
sonos: jayayaysan-u ečüs mayad ebderemüi-ja⁴, ‖ törökü bui ele bögesü
mayad ükükü bui⁵; nigültü kilinča üiledbesü, amitan tamu-dur unayu,
buyan üiledbesü degedü sain ‖ töröl-dür töröyü; yerü törökü ba ükükü
20 anu qamuγ bügüde-dür bui atala⁶, γayčaqan minu tula(da) ta bügüdeger
maši yekede ülü ‖ jobaγdaqu; bi ene metü sain töröl oluysan-dur ta
ber dayan bayasulčayad, buyan-u jüg-tür kičiyegdeküi. öd ügei ‖ γašiγun*

---

¹ *tngris-un ... šinjilen,* 'regarding the five existences with the eyes of
a god'.
² *oytaryui-bar ... baiju,* 'came via heaven, and stopped in the sky above'.
³ *mandur jarliγ boluγdaqui,* passive imperative, 'deign to speak to us'.
⁴ *jayayaysan-u ... ebderemüi ja,* 'the purpose of being created is, verily,
to be destroyed'.
⁵ *törökü bui ... ükükü bui,* 'what is born, whatever it be, is certainly that
which dies'. The idea is that we are all born and we all must die.
⁶ *törökü ... bui atala,* 'to be born and to die are something for everybody
(to do)'.

*jobalang yayun kereg' kemen ögülegsen-dür, ečige eke qoyar ögülerün
'ai köbegün či yeke nigüleskü̈i sedkil-iyer beyeben* ‖ *bars-tur öggüged,*
25 *qamuy bügüdeger-i nigüleskü̈i bui ele bögesü[7], edüge biden-i tebčiged
ügei boluysan-dur, bide čima-yi sanaju* ‖ *miqan-iyan oytaluysan metü
joban atala, ai yeke nigülesügči mani yayun-u tula tebčimüi?'.*

tedü̈i basa (tere) tngri-yin köbegün ‖ *eldeb sain üges-iyer eč̈ige eke
terigüten bügüde-yi sergügegsen-dür, eč̈ige eke anu üč̈ügen sergüged,*
30 *doloyan jü̈il erdinis-*‖*-iyer abdura kijü, yasun-i anu (tere) abdura
dotora oroyulju yajar-tur niyuyad, degere inu suburyan bosqabai. tngri-*‖
*-yin köbegün ber oron-dur-iyan qaribai. qayan qatun nököd selte bü-
güdeger ordu qarši-dur-iyan irebei.*

Vocabulary 10

abdura(n) box, container
bayasulča- to rejoice with one
  another
bosqa- to erect, raise
buyan good deed
bügüdeger all together

činggis Jengis
dayan also
degedü high, elevated
degegši upwards
degere above, upper, overhead
ebdere- to perish, ruin
ečüs end, purpose
eldeb diverse, various
ele bögesü whatever it may be, at
  all; if
enel- to sorrow, grieve
erdeni jewel
yayča one, only, sole
  yayčaqan only, sole
yasal- to complain
yašiyun bitter
jayaya- to create, bestow
  jayayan existence, fate, life
jiya- to show, teach
joba- to suffer, sorrow
  jobalang sorrow, suffering
jü̈il type, sort, kind
kičiye- to strive for
kilinča sin, fault

küriyelegül- to be surrounded,
  encircled
morila- to ride
nasu(n) age, years of life
nidü(n) eye
nigülesügči či man-u
  compassionate one
nigüleskü̈i compassion, pity
nigültü sinful
niyu- to hide, secrete
oytal- to chop to pieces
oytaryui heaven, sky
öd ügei bad, useless
qarši castle; palace
  ordu qarši court
qoni(n) sheep
  qoniči shepherd
  qonitu sheepowner
saišiya- to approve
saiqan pretty, beautiful
sergü- to be consoled
sergüge- to console, cheer up
suburyan pagoda, shrine
šinjile- to regard, investigate
tamu hell
tebči- to release, leave, get away
tegüs perfect, complete
t(e)ngri god; heaven
todqur danger, evil, misfortune
ügei bol- to die
yerü moreover, furthermore, in
  general

---

[7] *qamuy ... bögesü*, 'though it be everyone has commiseration', i.e., we
all understand why you did this.

III. Reader

A. Texts in Transcription

VII. The Good and the Bad King*

*urida nigen oron-a ečige köbegün qoyar aysan-ača ečige anu ükükü̈-degen
jakiju, 'köbegün minu, edüge ečige činu bi ükükü tula köbegün či ber
sain noyan-i šitüjü, sain kümün-lüge qanila, mayu kümün-lüge buu
nöküče' kemen jakijuqui. qoina tere köbegün ber tengsekü-yin tula[1]*
5 *nigen mayu qayan-i šitüged, tüšimel anu bolju yabun, nigen mayu
gergei abubai.* ‖
*tegünče qayan-luya qoyayula oi dotora yabutala, nigen baras qayan-u
emüne-eče ösürjü iregsen-dü, tere kümün ildü-ber tere baras-yi čabčiju
alaysan-du, tegün-dü qayan anu yekede bayarlaju jarliy bolurun,*
10 *'tüšimel, či minu amin-i aburaysan yeke ačitu kümün bolbai' kemeged,
tendeče tere tüšimel, qayan-u uidqar-i sergügekü nigen büjigči toyos
šibayun-i qulayuju nigen ekener-tür niyuju qadayalayuluyad, basa
nigen toyos[2] šibayun-i abču gertegen ireged, gergei-‖-degen niyuju
ögülerün, 'ene qayan-i bi ami aburaju tere metü ačilaysan bui bolbaču,*
15 *minu ači-yi tuqai ülü sanaqu tula, qayan-u ene toyos šibayun-i alaju
idesügei' kemen alaju ere eme qoyayula miqa-yi idebei.*
*tere tuqai-du qayan ber 'minu toyos šibayun-i ken kümün oluysan
bolbasu tere kümün-dü yeke šang šangnamui' kemen jarlaysan-du, tere
tüšimel-ün gergei anu qayan-du uridaki učir-i medegülügsen-dü qayan*
20 *jarliy bayulyan tere tüšimel-i dayudaju asayurun, 'či minu* ‖ *qairatai
toyos šibayun-i alaju idegsen ünen buyu[3] kemekü̈-dü, tere tüšimel
ailadqaju 'ünen bülüge' kemen uridu yabudal-i ögülegsen-dü, tegün-dü
qayan ber 'albatu inu ejen-degen kündülel üiledügsen-dü, ači-yi qariyulqu
yambar yeke kereg? egün-i ala' kemegsen-dü, tegünče tüšimel anu*
25 *qayan gergei qoyayula-yin mayu-yi medeged, qayan-u toyos šibayun-i
tušiyaju ögüged, öber-e busu oron-a yabubai.*
tendeče ögere nigen sain qayan-u tüšimel boluyad, ‖ *nigen mayu gergei
abču qanilayad, qayan tüšimel qoyayula oi-dur yabuysayar nigen usun
üigei yajar-a qayan kürčü qalayučaju yadaran yekede umdayasuysan-du*
30 *tegün-dü tüšimel ber 'tngri metü ejen, joyoylaju bolqu bolbasu[4] nadur*

---

* *Subhāṣita*, MS *Köke Qoto*, II. fol. 1 v. ff. Mongol Coll. Royal Libr. Copenhagen.

[1] *tengsekü-yin tula*, 'for purposes of comparison'.
[2] *basa nigen toyos*, i.e., another (different) bird.
[3] *buyu < bui + u*, 'Is it (true that . . .)?'
[4] *joyoylaju bolqu bolbasu*, 'if you are able to consume (anything)'. The use
of *bol-* with a form in *-ju* gives the meaning 'to be able to . . .'.

*γurban doloγoyna bainam' kemeged, ergügsen-dü, qayan yekede bayarlaǰu
joγoylaγad, 'meküs kümün-ü ami-yi aburaysan yeke ačitai bolbai',
kemebei.*

tere tüšimel qoina qayan-u köbegün-i nigen γaǰar niγuyad emüsügsen
35 *qubčasu čimeg-i ger-tegen abčiǰu ‖ gergei-degen ögülerün, 'ene anu qan
köbegün-ü qubčasu čimeg bülüge', dalda niγuǰu talbiγulbai.*

*tegünče
qayan yayaran 'minu köbegün-i oluysan kümün-e yeke šang kešig
ögüye' kemen ǰarlaysan-du, tere tüšimel-ün gergei anu, qan köbegün-ü
qubčasu čimeg-i abčiǰu qayan-du ailadqarun, 'činu tüšimel qan köbegün-i*
40 *alaγad qubčasu čimeg bükün anu ene bui' kemegsen-dü, qayan ǰarliγ
bayulγaǰu tüšimel-i dayudaǰu ögülerün, 'či yaγun-u tula minu köbegün-i
‖ alabai' kemeküi-dü, tüšimel ailadqarun, 'minu ači-yi ese sanaysan-u
tula könügebei' kemeküi-dü, qayan ǰarliγ bolurun, 'tüšimel či, yambar
ači tusa bui' kemeküi-dü, tüšimel ailadqarun, umdayasuǰu yadaraqui-du*
45 *doloγoyna bariysan-iyan ailadqaysan-du, qayan ǰöbšiyeǰü 'tere ünen
bülüge, teimü-yin tula minu köbegün nadur mašida qairatai tula, nigen
doloγoyna-yin qariyu boltuyai. qoyarduyar-un qariyu-dur bi keüken-
-iyen čimadur gergei bolyan ögsügei. γurbaduyar-un qariyu-dur minu
törö-yin ‖ qayas-i ögüye' kemegsen-dü, tüšimel kešig-tür mörgöǰü*
50 *ailadqarun, 'tngri metü boyda eǰen maši üčügen kündülel üiledügsen-dür
qariyu ačilaqu-yi sanaǰu yayakin bolqu bui, degedü qan köbegün-i ayul
ügei yayun-u tula qoorlaqu bui⁵' kemeged, yayaran qan köbegün-i abču
ireǰü, qayan-du ergügsen-dü, qayan yekede bayarlaǰu 'šangnai-a'
kemeküi-dü, tüšimel tedeger šang-yi ču abuysan ügei, ketürkei qayan-du*
55 *bučaγaǰu ergüged, tere tüšimel nigen nasun-du qayan-u ‖ törö-dür
ǰidküǰü kündülel-i üiledbei.*

VIII. The Brahman and the Goat*

*nigen biraman ber tngri-yi takiqu-yin tula imaγan qudalduǰu abuyad
kötölǰü yabuqui-yi [üǰeged] tere γaǰar-un tabun qulaγaiči kümün arya
kelelčeǰü, biraman-u odqu ǰam-dur nige ber yabuqu metü baiysan-ača¹
biraman ber yabuysayar angqan-u kümün-i dayariǰu γarqui-dur tere*
5 *qulaγaiči ber, 'ai-a yirtinčü-dür² noqai kötelügsen biraman ču bui
aǰuyu' kemen aliyalaqui metü ögüleküi-dür biraman ber kereg-tür abul
ügei³ yabubai. qoyaduyar qulaγaiči-luγa učiraqui-dur 'sain noqai
bainam' kemeged odbai. γutayar ba dötöger kümün ču tegünčilen ögüleküi-
-dür biraman sešig töröǰü imaγa-ban saitur ergičegülǰü üǰebesü, 'noqai-dur*

---

⁵ *tngri metü ... qoorlaqu bui.* Freely: How could the heavenly sacred
master think of bestowing reward on one who displayed so very little
respect? How could anyone brazenly dispose of the exalted prince?

Selection VIII.

* *Subhāṣita* 6, fol. 4 v.

¹ *yabuqu metü baiysan-ača*, 'pretending he was travelling'.
² *'ai-a yirtinčü dür ...'*, 'Lo, what in the world is it but a Brahman ...'.
³ *abul ügei*, 'taking no (notice)'.

10 *baiday urtu segül kimusu terigüten ügei böged, imayan-dur baiday eber*
ba eregün-ü saqal terigüten baiqu tula imaya mön' kemen sanayad
yabubai. tabuduyar qulayaiči ber üjegseger 'ai yambar sürekei noqai
bui' kemen sočigsan metü jailaju yarbai. tegün-e biraman ber, 'egün-i
učiraysan kümün bügüde noqai kemeldüküi-ber šinjilebesü⁴ ende-eče
15 *busu ulus-tur noqai ‖ üjegdekü bolbaču minu nidün-dür imaya bolju*
üjegdedeg ajuyu. mayad nigen yakša ber minu takil-i ideküi-yin tula
qubiluysan bolultai' kemen bodoyad imayan-iyan orkiyad yabuysan-u
darui⁵ qulayaičinar čuylaju imayan-i abačiyad idelüge.

IX. The Sharp-witted Daughter-in-law*

tere čay-tur Gegen-e Ilayuysan¹ qayan-dur Görügesün neretü nigen
tüšimel bülüge. tere tüšimel maši yeke ed ayurasu-tu bayan bülüge.
tere tüšimel-dür doloyan köbegün bülüge.

jiryuyan köbegün anu eme-yügen abuyad, odqan köbegün inu eme ese
5 *abuysan-dur, ečige anu ein sedkirün: 'edüge bi öteljü üküküi-dür oira*
bolbai. ene odqan köbegün-dür-iyen nigen sain ökin erijü ögsügei'
kemen sedkijü bürün, tere čay-tur tere tüšimel-dür nigen amaray biraman
bui. tere biraman-luya učiraju üge-yin ‖ ulam-ača duraduyad², biraman-
-dur ögülerün: 'ai biraman minu, ene odqan köbegün-dür eme ese yuiju
10 *bülüge. edüge ken-eče yuiqui ese medebei. ai biraman či qamuy ulus-tur*
oduyad minu köbegün-luya buyan kešig ibegel-tü mergen oyutu yooa
üjesküleng-tü teimü nigen ökin-i šinjilejü üjeged minu ene köbegün-dür
yuisuyai. čimayi bi ačilasuyai' kemen ögülegsen-dür, tere biraman:
'tein boltuyai' kemen ögüleged qamuy ulus-tur erire oduysan-dur, Širi
15 *Tigta neretü ulus-tur tabun jayun ökid qamtu nayaduyad, sain čečeg-*
-üd-i tegüged burqan-i takin büküi üjebei.

tere biraman anu tere ökid-i qamiya odbasu, qoina-ača inu dayaju üjebesü,
nigen üčügen usun-dur kürügsen-dür, tedeger qamuy ökid yutul-iyan
tailju usun-i getülbei. teden-ü dotora nigen ökin yutul-iyan ülü tailun
20 *yutul-tai getülbei. basa činayši odun atala, nigen mören-dür kürügsen-dür,*
busu qamuy ökid debel-iyen tailju usun-i getülbesü uridu tere ökin
debel-iyen ülü tailun getülbei. tegün-eče činayši nigen modun-u oi-dur
kürügsen-dür, busud ökid modun degere abariju čečeg abubai. uridu tere
ökin kösüre-eče čečeg tegüjü busud-ača ülemji olbai. uridu tere
25 *tedüi tere biraman tere ökin-ü dergede oduyad ein ögülerün: 'ai ökin*

---

⁴ *šinjilebesü*, 'even when I investigated it'.
⁵ *yabuysan-u darui*, 'as soon as he had travelled on'.

Selection IX.

* Xyl. *Üliger-ün dalai*, fol. 103r21 to 105v28.

¹ *Gegen-e Ilayuysan*, 'having surpassed (all others) in splendor' is the *qayan's*
name.

² *üge-yin ulam-ača duraduyad*, during the course of the conversation.

³ *čima-ača nigen sešig asayqu bülüge*, 'there was the asking of a doubt from
you', i.e., there was something I wanted to ask you about.

čima-ača nigen sešig asayqu bülüge³. či saitur qariyu ögülegdeküi' kemen
ögülegsen-dür, ökin ögülerün: 'čimadur yambar sešig bui ele bögesü
asayuydaqui' kemen ögülegsen-dür, biraman ögülerün: 'ai ökin ta usun
getülküi-dür busu ökid yutul-iyan tailju getülbesü, či ∥ yayčayar yutul-
30 -tai getülküi šiltayan činu yayun bui?' ökin ögülerün: 'ai biraman,
činu tere sešig yeke yaiqamšiy busu bolai. ai biraman bi qayurai yajar-tur
yabuqui čay-tur nidün-iyer üjejü ürgüsün ba, čilayun ba, toyosqa ba,
teimü mayu-yi üjejü jailaju yabuqu bülüge. ker-be usun dotora ürgüsün
ba, moyai ba, qoor-tu qoroqai bui ele bögesü ülü üjen gičkibesü⁴, köl-dür
35 qoor-tu bolumui⁵ kemen sedkijü, yutul-iyan ese tailuysan tere bülüge'.
biraman ögülerün: 'busud ökin debel-iyen šiyuju usun-ača getülbesü.
či yayčayar debel-iyen ülü šiyun getülkü yayun bui?' kemen asaybasu,
ökin ögülerün: 'ökin kümün-ü beye-dür⁶ sain mayu belge olan bükü-yin
tula, debel-iyen šiyuju orobasu, busud kümün sain belge-yi üjebesü
40 yayun ber ülü ögülemü; mayu belge-yi üjebesü eleglekü-yin tulada,
minu debel-iyen ese šiyuysan tere bülüge'.
biraman ögülerün: 'tein ber bögesü busu ökid modun degere abariju
čečeg tegün atala, či yayčayar modun-dur ülü abariqu šiltayan yayun
bui?' kemen asaybasu, ökin ögülerün: 'ker-be modun degere abaribasu,
45 modun-u gešigün quyuraju kösür-e unabasu, beyen-dür qoor bolqu-yin
tula, modun-dur ese abariysan minu tere bülüge'.
tere ökin-ü ečige anu Gegegen-e Ilayuyči qayan-u degü bülüge. tere
qayan-u degü inu urida nigen gem kigsen-dür, tere ulus-ača üldegdejü
ende ireged, Lamčam-ma ökin abču törögsen köbegün bui ajuyu.
50 tere biraman ökin-dür ögülerün: 'ai ökin či maši šiluyun uqayatu
bögetele čimadur ečige eke buyu?' kemen asaybasu, ∥ ökin ögülerün:
'ečige eke bui' kemegsen-dür, biraman ögülerün: 'tein ber bögesü bi
čimaluya qamtu činu ger-tür odsuyai' kemen qanilaju oduyad, qayalya-
-dur kürügsen-dür, ökin gertegen oroyad ečige eke-degen ögülerün:
55 'biden-ü qayalya-dur nigen biraman ireged, čimadur jolyasu⁷ kemen
sayun amui'. ečige inu yadan-a yarču tanilduyad esen mendü-yügen
asayulčayad, biraman ögülerün: 'Saiki ökin činukei buyu?' kemen
asaybasu, 'minu ökin bui' kemen ögülegsen-dür, biraman ögülerün:
'teimü bögesü kümün yuyuysan buyu?' kemen asaybasu, 'yuyuysan
60 ügei bülüge' kemen ögülebei. biraman ögülerün: 'teimü bögesü Širavast
balyasun-daki Görügesün neretü tüšimel-i či tanimuu?' kemen asaybasu,
tere kümün ögülerün: 'bide qoyar uruy bülüge' kemen ögülegsen-dür,
biraman ögülerün: 'tere tüšimel-dür doloyan köbegün bülüge. tegün-ü
dotora odqan köbegün inu yooa üjesküleng-tü buyu. tegün-dür činu
65 ökin-i yuyubasu ögümü⁸?' tere kümün ögülerün: 'tere tüšimel yeke
sain ijayur-tu bülüge. ker-be ökin-i minu yuyuqu bögesu, činu üge-ber
ögsügei' kemen ögülegsen-dür, tere biraman qariju ireged šiltayan učir

---

⁴ ülü üjen kičkibesü, 'if one does not see the ... and steps on (them)'.
⁵ köl-dür qoor-tu bolumui, it is hard on the feet.
⁶ ökin kümün-ü beye-dür, 'because a girl-person's body has ...'.
⁷ čimadur jolyasu, he would (like to) visit you.
⁸ ögümü, interrogative form.

bügüde-yi delgerengküi-e tere Görügesün neretü tüšimel-dür ögülegsen-dür,
tedüi tere tüšimel beri-yügen abqui morin terge terigüten-i beledüged,
70 *öber-iyen nököd selte bügüdeger, Širi-Tigta neretü ulus qamiya bükü*
tende odbai.

tere ulus-tur oiratuysan-dur, 'nigen kümün-i urid ilegeye' kemen sedkiǰü,
tere kümün-i ein ǰakirun: 'ai kümün či urid oduyad, ökin-ü ečige
eke-dür ‖ *'bide bügüdeger aisui*[9]*' kemen sonosqaydaqui'; tere kümün*
75 *kürüged sonosqayuluysan-dur, tedüi tere kümün*[10] *ayui yeke qorim*
beledüged ökin-iyen bayulyaǰu ögsügei kemen ǰabdubai.

tedüi darui deger-e bügüdeger kürčü ireged, činayši inayši qorimlalduǰu
ökin-i inu bayulyaǰu abču iredüi-dür, tere ökin-ü eke anu olan kümün-ü
dotora ökin-iyen ein suryarun: 'ai ökin minu či ene edür-eče qoinayšida
80 *nasu turqaru sain degel emüsüged, sain amtatu idegen idegdeküi; edür*
büri tasural ügei tolin-dur-iyan üǰegdeküi' kemen suryaysan-dur, ökin
ber 'tein kisügei' kemen ögülegsen-dür, qadum ečige eke inu tayalan ein
sedkirün: 'kümün nigen nasun degere ǰobalang ǰiryalang ber mönyke
busu bögetele[11]*, nasun turqaru sain debel sain idegen qamiya-ača oldamui?*
85 *ürgülǰide tolin-dur üǰebesü ber kereg inu yayun*[12]*?' kemen sedkibei.*
tedüi esergü tesergü dailaldun qorimlayad tarqabai.

tedüi tere bügüde mör-tür oroǰu qariǰu ireküi-dür ǰayura nigen sain
serigün baišing bui aǰuyu[13]*. urida qadum ečige inu tere baišing-dur*
kürüged yaiqan sayun aǰuyu. šini beri inu qoina-ača ireged, qadum
90 *ečige-degen ein öčirün: 'ene baišing-dur sayuǰu ülü bolumu*[14]*. ödter*
böged yadana ögede bolun soyorqa' kemen öčibesü. tedüi beri-yügen
üge-ber yadana yarbai. nigen kedün kümün yadana ülü yarun sayun
büküi-dür qorumqan ǰayura morin üker baišing-un bayanas-i širgü-
gegsen-dür baišing unayad, dotora sayuysan kümün anu ükübei. qadum
95 *ečige anu ein sedkirün: 'namayi ber ǰobalang-un aman-ača ene beri*
minu yaryabai' kemen sedkiǰü, ‖ *beri-yügen ülemǰi asaran qairalabai.*

basa tendeče yabutala, usun ebesün tegüsügsen nigen yool-dur sayun
atala, beri inu qoina-ača kürčü ireged, 'ene yool-dur sayuǰu ülü bolumu.
ödter-e ǰögegdeküi' kemen ögülebesü, beri-yügen üge-ber nigen eteged
100 *ǰögeǰü sayun atala, yeke türgen qura oroyad, yool dügüreng yeke üyer*
boluysan-dur, qadum ečige inu ein sedkirün: 'ene beri minu namayi
qoyar üküleng-eče tonilyabai' kemen sedkibei.

---

[9] *aisui*, archaic durative form in *-u(i)*, 'we are approaching'.
[10] *kümün* = *ečige*.
[11] *kümün nigen . . . busu bögetele*, 'Although a man is not eternally in (either)
sorrow or rejoicing during his lifetime', i.e., everyone has his ups and
downs.
[12] *kereg inu yayun?* Of what use is it to . . .?
[13] *nigen . . . baišing bui aǰuyu*, lit. 'there existed a house', freely, 'they
came upon a house'.
[14] *ene baišing-dur sayuǰu ülü bolumu*, 'this house is not to be sat in' (lit. do
not be one sitting in this house').
[15] *nigen edür dayustala*, until a day had passed.

basa tendeče yabuyad yajar-tur-iyan kürčü ireged sača, qamuy uruy
tariy bügüdeger nigen edür dayustala[15] *qorim kijü nayadun bayasbai.*
105 *jočid-i tarqaysan-u qoina beriyed-iyen quriyaju ireged, ein ögülerün:*
'edüge bi öteljü üiles jakirču ülü čidamui. ed tavar üile bügüde-yügen
tan-dur qadayalayulun ögsügei. tülkigür onisun-i ken qadayalamu?'
kemen asaybasu, jiryuyan beri inu 'bide qadayalaju ülü čidam' kemen
öčigsen-dür, odqan beri inu 'bi qadayalaju čidamui' kemen öčibesü,
110 *tedüi tere ger-ün ejen onisun tülkigür bügüde-yi tegün-dur ögbei; üiles-i*
jakirayal(a)yulbai. tere beri inu manayar büri erte bosuyad, qarši
baišing-i arčiyad, usun ösürčü tendeče eldeb idegen-i beledüged, urida
qadum ečige eke-degen ögüged, tegün-ü qoina yeke baya-dur jergeber
ögüged, tegün-u qoina boyol šibegčin-dür ögüged üiles-i jakiruyad, tende
115 *ber öber-iyen idejüküi.*

The above text represents about one-fourth of the story.

B. The Mongolian Script

Mongolian Numerals.

Mongolian blockprints (xylographs) rarely use the Mongolian numerals.
Instead, the numbers are fully written out in words, whether in the
body of the text, or in the pagination at the left side, hence, *jayun*
döčin qoyar "142". Many Peking blockprints also bear the numbers in
Chinese figures.

When Mongolian numerals occur in a sentence in vertical script, as in
a letter or a manuscript, they are given from left to right, and stand
upright as in the list that follows. However, for typographical reasons,
in modern books and on the Mongolian typewriter, the Mongolian
numerals are turned 90° so that they will not protrude beyond the rest
of the line.

The Mongolian figures are written from left to right, as Arabic figures:

1	2	3	4	5	6	7	8	9	0
Ɉ	*ᘀ*	*ᘁ*	*Ɗ*	*ᗷ*	*ᗿ*	*ᔮ*	*Ɩ*	*ℓ*	*0*

Mongolian Script.

The Mongolian script is written vertically, and read from top to bottom,
the lines proceeding from left to right. Words written in the native
script resemble a series of notches broken by loops and strokes. There
are no capital letters or punctuation marks such as our question
mark or quotation mark—only a mark denoting the end of a clause

and the end of a paragraph, and even these are often negligently employed.

Manuscripts, xylographs (wood-block prints) and printed books may use the Mongolian figures for numbers, but more often they will spell out the number in words, as *ǰayun döčin qoyar*, 142. Most modern books are paginated with Arabic numbers.

The basic (or medial) form of the letters should be learned first. It then becomes clear that the initial and final forms are slight variants with hooks and flourishes.

The fact cannot be disguised that the script is ambiguous. The vowels *a / e*, *o / u*, *ö / ü* and the consonants *k / g*, *q / γ*, *t / d* are not clearly differentiated in all positions. Consequently, a word like can be read *urtu*, long, or *ordu*, palace, depending on the context. There is no ambiguity from the Mongol's point of view, as the context makes it clear, just as English *read* (present) and *read* (past) are not confused.

After the student has seen some familiar words in the native script, such as *nigen*, *qayan*, *tere*, *köbegün*, he will begin to remember word-pictures. Common endings such as *-dur*, *-gsen*, *-iyen*, *-bai*, soon become second nature, and the only problem is to decide about *o / u*, *t / d*, etc.

The basic (medial) forms should be thoroughly memorized, and the remaining remarks about individual variations in letters should be carefully studied. Then the student may begin a story in Mongolian script, referring to the transcription as necessary. Acquisition of fluency is then merely a matter of reading additional texts. It is true that there are editions of modern dialect texts in European phonetic script by European philologists, and for the use of Mongols on Russian territory new Cyrillic alphabets have been created. But for all work in Mongolian classical literature, and for use of dictionaries, its mastery remains a *sine qua non*.

I. *Vowels.*

Words beginning with a vowel may not do so unaided, but require a prefixed ◢ (like the Arabic *alif*, or the Hebrew *aleph*). The vowel *e* is not written initially, and only the *alif* indicates its presence (giving the appearance that initial *e* requires no *alif*). The mid vowels *ö* and *ü* require the stroke of the *i* ◄ added under the ◢, to form ฯ. When *ö / ü* are not the first letter or in the first syllable of a word, this stroke is omitted, as vowel harmony shows whether *o / u* or *ö / ü* is to be read.

Final forms. After a consonant, final *-a / -e* extends the hook ◢ with a stroke to ◣, or may use a flourish in the opposite direction, thus, ◥.

Final *i* rounds off the form ◄ to ♡. Final *o*/*u*, *ö*/*ü* bring the stroke of ↲ around to ◐.

Diphthongs. A diphthong in which *i* is always the second element, as in a word like *sain*, good, may be written in two ways, *saain* (*sa'in*), or *saiin* (*sayin*) 𝕀. The latter graph is found in all xylographs and ancient manuscripts, the former prevails in more recent manuscripts. These words may be transcribed either as *sain* or *sayin*, *teimü* or *teyimü* etc. Other combinations of two or more vowels are not diphthongs and are written in a normal manner: *keüken*, child; *taulai*, hare; *γooa*, beautiful; *činua-yi*, wolf (acc.), etc.
Note that the diphthongs *oi*, *ui*, and *üi* coincide in 𝖆. Do not confuse this with 𝖆, which is *ö*/*ü*.

II. *Consonants.*

n. The point of *n* is often omitted, especially when it occurs after a vowel. The point often stands one stroke farther down, as it is added afterwards, like dotting an i. Final *n* is lengthened, cf. *a*.

q/*γ.* The round stroke of ⟩ becomes medially a doubled hook. Analyse the word 𝖆 𝖆 *aqa*, elder brother: 1. initial *alif* 2. vowel *a* 3. double hook of *q* 4. final *-a*, extended. Medially, the points of *γ* are often omitted, or stand one stroke removed.

b. *b* ◐ will not be confused with (final) *o*/*u*, as *b* occurs after a vowel, and *o*/*u* after a consonant. Final *b* has the form ◞. The syllable *bo*/*bu* has the ligature ℬ.

In foreign words, the unvoiced *p* is indicated by adding a hook.

s/*š.* The addition of two points makes *s* to *š*. When *i* follows, *s* is always read *š*. At the end of a word another *s* occurs, especially in the xylographs, in the shape of a short final *n*. Cf. table p. 72.

t/*d.* Initially, the form is ↓. Medially, the forms ◄ and 𝖖 occur. The last given looks like *on*, but occurs only finally and before consonants.

𝖖 *qalaγun* but 𝕀 *sayuγad* 𝖆 *tende* ↗ *erdeni*

Since *l* has a final upward stroke and *m* a downward stroke, the combination *-ml-* must be written with a ligature, as in 𝖆. The final form of *-m* is ◄.

y/j. Since *j* does not occur in Uighur, there was no letter for it in the old alphabet. Initially it was written with *y* and medially with *č*. About 1700 a variant of the latter character was introduced for medial *j*, and in manuscripts from the 19th century initial *y* is distinguished from *j* by an upward tilt of the end of the stroke. This latter form is not found in the table p. 60, which only registers the letters found in the xylographs.

k/g. Following vowels are combined into the stroke. *ke/ge* is ⟲, *ki* is ⟲, *ko/go* (*ku/gu*) is ⟲, etc. The combination *ng* is simply *n* + *g*. Final *k/g* is a somewhat elongated ⟍.

⟲ *köbegün* ⟲ *bilig*

v. Easily confused with *y* and in many xylographs indistinguishable from it.

h. Only in foreign words. When initial, it requires a supporting *alif*.

Besides the normal alphabet there is a complete set of letters, distinguished by various diacritics, for the transcription of Tibetan and Sanskrit Buddhist terms, the so-called galik-letters, which were invented about the beginning of the 14th century. The letters *p*, *k* and *h* of the table p. 60 have been taken over from the galik-series. In manuscripts from South Mongolia Manchu-letters may also be met with.

Orthographical Conventions

Foreign words and names may violate all of the above practices, as well as beginning with several consonants, and ending in consonants which do not generally end words, and so on.

The double *oo* in words like *γool*, *qoor* and *door* is a mere conventional graph in certain words. So is the frequent doubling of a final round vowel, as in *buu*, not, and *degüü*, younger brother. Words which appear to contain diphthongs have generally lost an intervocalic *γ/g*. This is especially frequent in words containing another *γ/g* or *q/k*, e. g. *keüken*, *auya*. The emphatic final -*ja* is written -*i-a*.

When medial *d* and *g* must be shown unambiguously, they are written doubled, as in the word *qudduγ*, well, which would otherwise be identical with *qutuγ*, holy. The example most frequently met will be the forms of the verb *ög*-, to give, written always with two *g*'s before suffixes beginning with a vowel, as *öggügsen*, given. It would otherwise be indistinguishable from *ükü*-, to die, in forms like *ükügsen*, dead.

Some manuscripts and xylographs distinguish between -*tur* (with the letter for initial *t/d*) and -*dur* (with the medial *t/d*) in the dative-locative suffix.

A few Turkish loanwords have been taken over in their Uighur garb, such as *tngri = tengri*, *jrlγ = jarliγ*, *kkir = kir*.

Some scribes incline, in certain suffixes, to write only one of a front / back pair, the reader supplying the proper pronunciation instinctively, such as *aqa-yügen* (for *aqa-yuγan*), *eke-luya* (for *eke-lüge*) or *čečeg-nuγud* (for *čečeg-nügüd*).

The Mongolian Alphabet[1]

Number	Transcription	Characters		
		Initial	Medial	Final
1	*a*			
2	*e*			
3	*i*			
4	*o* *u*			
5	*ö* *ü*			
6	*n*			
7	*ng*			
8	*q*			
9	*γ*			
10	*b*			
11	*p*			
12	*s*			
13	*š*			
14	*t* *d*			
15	*l*			
16	*m*			
17	*č*			
18	*j*			
19	*y*			
20	*k* *g*			
21	*k*			
22	*r*			
23	*v*			
24	*h*			

[1] From N. Poppe, *Grammar of Written Mongolian*, Wiesbaden 1954, p. 17.

Plate I

Reading Exercise

Selection X

"The Wise Young Brahman"

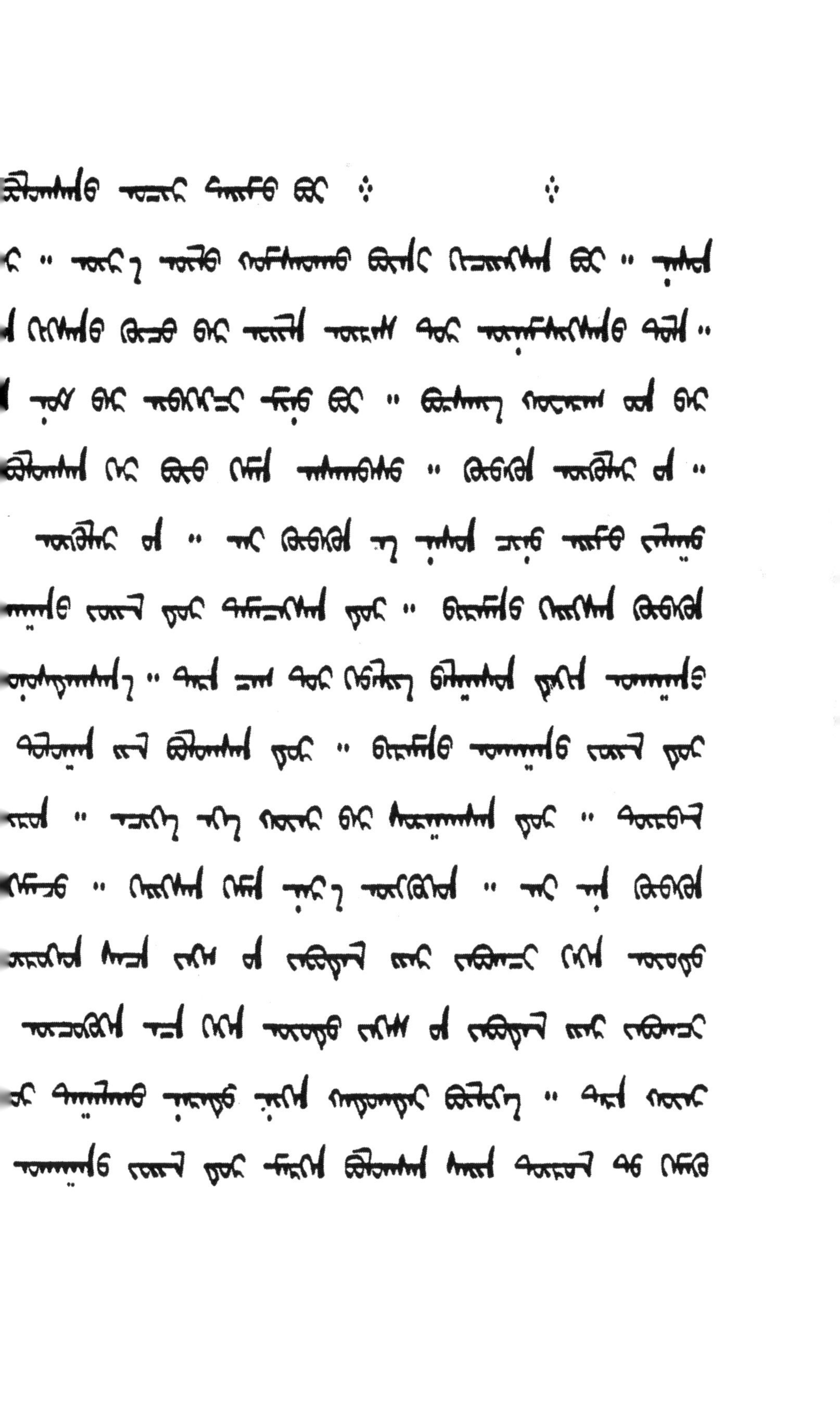

Transcription

X. "The Wise Young Brahman"*

erte urida Kabalik balyasun-dur biraman-u qamuy uqayan-u ǰüil-dür mergen boluysan Sain Töröl-tü kemekü ‖ nigen biraman bülüge. tere biraman-dur Sedkil-dur Tayalaqu neretü nigen qatuytai bülüge. tere qoyar-‖-ača nigen köbegün töröǰüküi. tere köbegün inu üčügüken-eče gegen oyutu yekes-ün yabudal-iyar yabuyči¹ ‖ nigen bolbai. tende eke inu 'aya ene köbegün töröged sača yekes-ün yabudal-iyar yabuyči gegen oyutu ‖ bükü-yin tula, mayad nigen ǰayaya-tu bui-ǰa' kemeǰü, Geigsen kemen nere öggüged, 'ai ene köbegün-‖-dür qamuy uqayan-u ǰüil-i suryasuyai' kemeǰü bürün, ečige eke qoyar ber suryaysan-dur, dörbel ‖ ügei medeküi nigen² bolbai. tere köbegün inu doloyan ǰil bo- luysan-dur, biraman-u uqayan-u ǰüil-dür ‖ mergen boluysan erdem-üd inu qamuy bügüdeger-tür sonostaysan-a, tere čay-tur Kabalik balyasun- -dakin uqayan-u ‖ ǰüil-dür mergen boluysan qamuy biraman čiyulǰu uqayan-u ǰüil-dür temečegsen-dür, biraman-u Geigsen köbegün ‖ maši yeke ülemǰi boluysan-dur, tedeger biraman ögülerün, 'ai köbegün a nasun činu eimü ǰalayu ‖ bögetele, uqayan-u ǰüil-dür ene metü mergen boluysan ker buyu' kemen asaybasu, köbegün ögülerün ‖ 'toyoluysan burqan ber bayši minu bui. boydas-un nom ber ibegegči minu bui. bursang quvaray-ud ber ‖ uduridduyči minu bui. yurban erdenis-ün adistid kigsen-ü küčü-ber üile üres-tür ünemšigsen-ü tula³, sešig ügei erte šiltayan-u köröngge sačaysan-dur, üre ülü qomsadqu buyan-i kičiyegsen bui⁴. nasun ‖ minu ǰalayu bolbasu, uqayan-u ǰüil-dür mergen boluysan-u učir teimü bui'.

---

* From I. J. Schmidt: *Grammatik der mongolischen Sprache*, St. Petersburg, 1831, p. 16.

¹ *gegen oyutu ... yabuyči*, 'he was one who went in the ways of the great ones of illuminated insight'.

² *dörbel ügei medeküi nigen*, 'one knowing no obstacle (to attain Nirvana)'.

³ *yurban erdenis-un ... ünemšigsen-ü tula*, 'because I have become aware of the consequences of action through the power of the three jewels blessing'.

⁴ *sešig ügei ... kiǰiyegsen bui*, 'when, free from doubt, I sowed the seed of original cause, I attained virtue of no small consequence'.

* * *

Persons who begin reading in Mongolian script at lesson 8 should first read plates II, III and IV. If you begin now with Plate I (Selection X), there are forms there which are not known by lesson 8.

Plate II

Selection XI

„The Hungry Tigress"[1]

[1] For transcription see lessons 8, 9 and 10.

Plate III

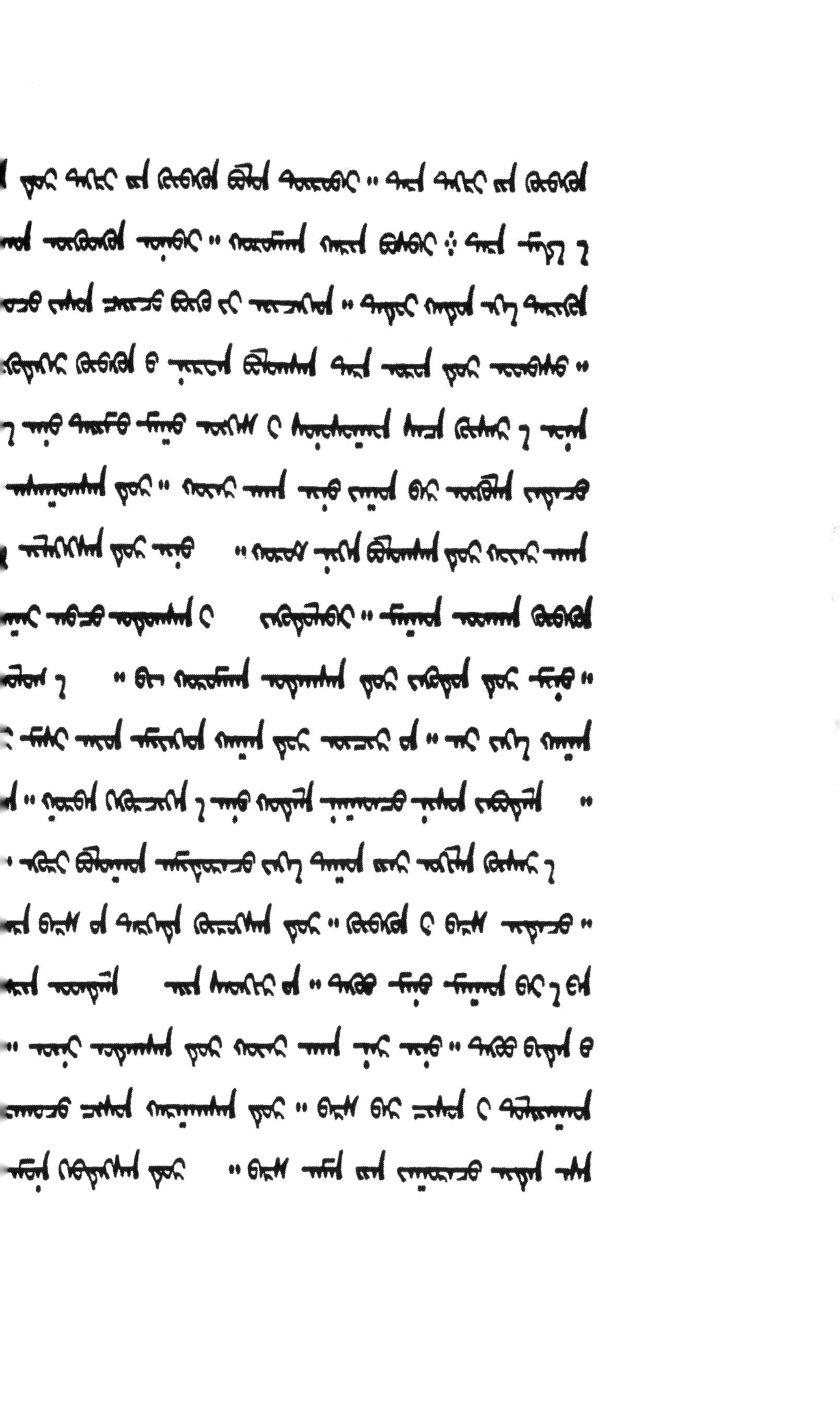

Plate IV

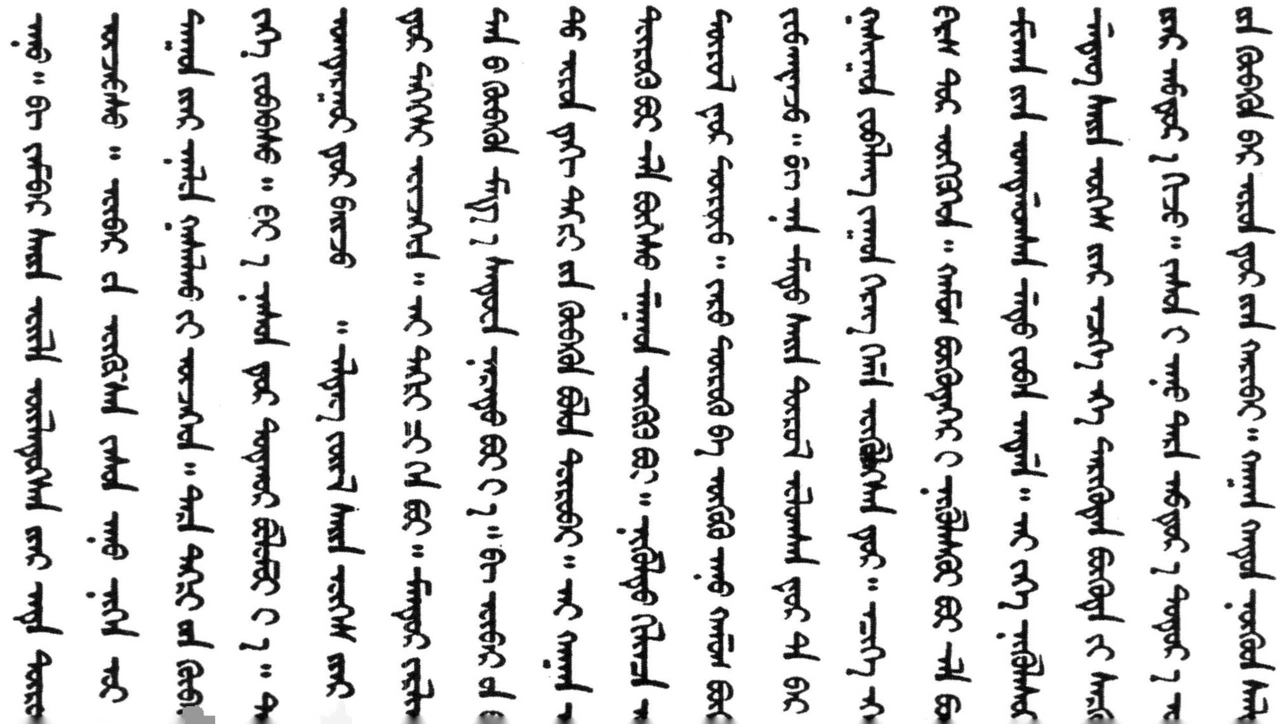

IV. Glossary

Mongolian-English Glossary

The glossary is intended to be complete for all words cited in the lessons and reading selections. The entries are mostly arranged to show common elements or derivative stems, where this does not unduly violate the alphabetical order. Verbs are entered under the stem form (*bol-*), but some common derived forms (*kemen, bögesü*) have also been entered. The more obvious loan-words are marked with the language of derivation. The plurals of many common words are entered.

The vocabularies of Lessons 1—10 contain about 500 words, and the reading selections, another 500. This glossary may also serve to read the selections in K. Grønbech, *Mongolske Tekster i Originalskrift*[1], Copenhagen, 1945.

The order of letters in the glossary is as follows: *a, b, č, e, γ, i, j/y, k/g, l, m, n, q, r, s, š, t/d, o/u, ö/ü*. This arrangement makes it possible to locate a word met either in transcription or in the original script by looking in only one place. While preserving the essential order of European alphabets, it also prepares the student to use Mongolian dictionaries.

Minor variations in spelling, as *a/i, a/u*, etc., are seldom given an additional listing in the glossary. The complete range of meanings for a word is not always given, but the definitions are restricted to those suitable to the stories.

A

a voc. part., Oh!, Ah! (see § 44 d)
a- to be
ab- to take, to buy, to take in marriage
abču ire- to bring
abači- to take, take away; conduct
abaγai a form of address to one's elders; sire
abari- to mount, climb up
abčira- to bring, fetch
abiyas inclination, habit, nature
abqaγul- to have take
abdara|n, abdura|n box, container

abulča- to take (with one another); to fight (one another)
abura- to save, rescue, protect
abural protection
ači good deed; benefaction
ači tusa reward
ačila- to show mercy; to reward
ačitu possessing virtue; charitabel
aγali custom; character; habit
aγaši movement; form; conduct
aγta gelding
aγui very, great, vast
aγul- to place, put, arrange
aγula|n mountain

---

[1] Specifically, these are the frame story, story 1 (the tale of the rich man's son) and story 8 (the tale of the painter and the joiner) from the Tales of Siddhi Kür (the Vetālapañcaviṃçatika), Chapter 34 (the tale of the good and the bad prince) from the *üliger-ün dalai* (The Sea of Stories), and pp. 62—70 of I. J. Schmidt's edition of Saγang Sečen's Chronicle.

aɣulja- to meet; to visit
aɣuljar meeting; corner, end
aɣur air; spirit; force
aɣurla- be angry
aɣurasun things, goods
   aɣurasutu having possessions, rich
ai voc. part., Oh!, Ah! (see § 44 d)
aia (*aya*) voc. part., Oh!, Ah! (see § 44 d)
ail camp; neighbourhood
ailadqa- to report; to say (to a superior)
aisu- to approach
ajai, aji = *ajuɣu*
ajuɣu was (see § 49 a)
ala- to kill
   alaldu- to fight (one another)
alaɣ variegated, of various colors
alaɣul- to have kill
alba|n tax, tribute; duty, obligatory service
   albatu subject, slave
alɣur slow, quiet, careful
ali what, where
   ali ... *ali* either ... or
   ali ba every, any
   ali büri anyone, no one
   ali ken anyone, who, he who
   ali yaɣun anything
alin who, which (of several)
aliya prank, jest
   aliyala- to joke, play pranks
aljiya- to be tired
alqu step, pace
alda- to drop; lose; sin, lack, fail to attain
   aman alda- to promise
alta|n gold
aldaɣul- to abandon, flee; to make sin
aldar glory, fame, honour
aldarši- to become famous
aldartan said (pl.) famous persons, celebrities
aldara- to leave, abandon, become detached
aluqa hammer
alurqai slope, bending
alus (postposed), across, through
ama|n 1. mouth, lips, opening
   2. family, household
amaraɣ friend; dear, well-loved

amaraqla- to love passionately
amiri (Skt.) mango
ami|n spirit, breath, life
amitu one possessing life, a being
   amitan (pl.) living beings
amidura- to live; to come to oneself
amta|n taste, good taste
amu- to be peaceful, happy; to rest
   amuɣul- to calm, pacify, make happy
   amuɣulang peace, happiness, calm
amui see *a-*
amur peace, happiness, fortune
   amurqan quite peaceful
amurči- to rest; to live in peace
   amurčiɣul- to pacify, calm
anggir 1. orange, yellow
   2. duck-like bird
angqa|n beginning, first
   angqaduɣar the first
anu nom. part., indicates preceding word is subject; his; see § 10
aqa elder brother
araki wine, brandy
   arakitu drunk
arasu|n skin, leather, hide
arad people, nation
arbai barley, oats
arban ten
arbičiɣul- to increase, grow
arbid- to be increased, enlarged
   arbidqa- to increase, enlarge (tr.)
arči- to clean
arya means; art, craft, plan; trick
   aryala- to scheme, employ cunning
   aryada- to ensnare, trap, ambush
   aryatu crafty, artful
aryamji cord, rope
aryul slow, gentle, peaceful
ariɣun pure, clean, sacred
ariki = *araki*
arilɣa- to clean, cleanse, cure; to vanquish (fear)
arsalan lion
aru back, spine, behind, north
arši (Skt.) a Rishi, a saint
asaɣ|u- to ask, inquire
   asaɣul question
   asaɣulča- to ask (one another)
asara- to have pity on, to commiserate; to bring up

asqa- to empty, pour out
asuru very, extremely, more
ašiɣla- to use, make use of
ašida always; constant, eternal
ataɣa|n envy, jealousy
    ataɣatu envious, jealous; evil minded
atala about to
adali (postposed) equal, like, similar
adistid (Skt.) blessing, providence
aduɣu|n herd (esp. of horses)
    aduɣula- to watch herd
    aduɣusu|n cattle, stock
aturiɣul- to wrinkle, pucker, frown
auɣa strength, might
aya (aia) voc. part., Oh!, Ah! (see § 44 d)
ayaɣ-qa takimlig (Uig.) a rank of priest, gelung
ayaɣa bowl, cup
ayu- to fear, dread
    ayul fright, fear

B

ba and, also; we
baɣa small; young
    baɣačud (pl.) children
    baɣa saɣa trifle; little by little
baɣana column; support
baɣatur hero (cf. Russ. богатырь); brave, courageous
baɣča package, bundle
bayši (Chin.?) teacher, scholar
baɣtaɣa- to contain, hold
baɣu- to descend, get down; to sit down
    baɣulɣa- to have descend, lower; to decree; to marry off
bai- to be, exist; to wait, dwell, stand
    baiɣul- to place, set, build, erect, establish
    bailɣa- to stop (tr.), discontinue
    baina|m is; being (durative of *bai-*)
    baidaɣ what customarily is; usual
    baidal state, manner, form
baišing (Chin.) building, house, room
bajaɣa- to arrange, prepare
balɣasu|n (pl. *balɣad*) city, town, village
bara- to finish, conclude, consume

baraɣda- to be finished, come to an end
    baraɣdaši ügei inexhaustible, endless
baraɣa merchandise; something in the distance; reality
baraɣada- to visit, have an audience
baraɣun right
bari- to take, seize, catch, keep
    bariɣul- to have take; to catch
    barildu- to hold one another, wrestle, fight
barkira- to cry, shout
bars, baras tiger
basa then, still, also
    basa ču (kü) again, once more
basu things, goods, riches
badara- to blaze, flame
    badaraɣul- to inflame, ignite; to increase
batu hard, firm, honest
bayan rich
bayar joy, happiness
    bayar üiles gifts
    bayarla- to rejoice, be happy
bayas- to be happy, rejoice
    bayasqulang joy, delight, rejoicing
    bayasulča- to rejoice (with one another)
bekile- to strengthen
belčir confluence of rivers
beleg (pl. *-üd*) gift, present
beled- to prepare, set up
belge (pl. *-s*) sign, mark
belkegüsü|n waist
ber nom. part., indicates preceding word is subject; makes pronouns indefinite; see § 10
bere mile
beri (pl. *beriyed*) daughter-in-law, (pl.) engaged couple
berke difficult; heavy
beder marks, figures, designs
beye self, body, nature
    beye minu I
bi I (see § 35)
biči- to write
    bičig writing, letter, composition, book
bičin monkey
bičiqan little, little bit
bilig knowledge

bing (Chin.) name of a year
biraman (Skt.) Brahman
bišire- to respect, worship
bide we (see § 35)
blama (Tib.) lama, priest
bširu (Tib.) coral
buča- to return, turn back
    bučaya- to return (tr.)
boyda holy, sacred
boyo- to bind, tie
    boyol slave, subject
bui is, there is; existing, being
    bui-ja there is indeed, there
    certainly is
bol- to be, become, exist, be possible
-ju bol- to be able
bolai = buyu
bula- to bury, plant
bulay source, spring
bolbaču although, if, in spite of
bolbai = bui
bolbasu if, as, when, in event
bolbasun finished (meal), prepared
    (food)
bolya- to make, do produce
bulya- to fight, assault, attack
bolyaya- to notice; to verify
buli- to take away (by force)
    buliya- to rob
    buliyayda- to be robbed, plundered
*bolja-*to arrange,make an appointment
boljaldu- to be arranged
boljimar, boljumur lark
bolda- to be; to make, accomplish
bolday|a hill
boltala up to, as far as, while, during
bultari- to shirk work
boluyujai perhaps
bolui (archaic) *= bolumui*
bolultai possible
bolumui is
bolor crystal, rock crystal
bolusa(i) conditional of *bol-*
boluyu = bolui
buqa bull, ox
buqar (Skt.) temple
burqan (ult. < Skt.) intelligence,
    supreme reason; Buddha
bursang quvaray (Uig.) union of
    priests, clergy
burtay filth
buruy color

buruyud- to blame; to flee
buruyula- to flee; to behave im-
    properly
burušiya- to reproach
bos- to arise, stand up
    bosqa- to make, stand; raise, erect,
    build
busu (pl. *-d*) 1. other, different
            2. not, without
busuyu = busu + u
bošoy word; order
buta thicket
bodi (Skt.) the perfection of intelli-
    gence to the Buddhistic state
bodo- to consider, regard; determine
budu- to paint
    buduy coloring, dye
budaya|n rice, millet; porridge
buu prohibitive part., negates im-
    peratives (see § 44 b)
buyan good deed, virtuous act
buyu 1. is; or (see § 49)
    2. *bui + u*, is it?
bü- (*bö-*) to be
    bögesü if, if there be, in event
    tein ber bögesü if that is the case
    bögetele as long as, inasmuch as
böge shaman
bögle- to stop up, cover
bügüde all, every, entire
    bügüdeger all, all together
böjig- to dance
    böjigči dancer
bükün (pl. of *büküi*) all, every(thing)
bülečeg ring
büliige (he) was; there was, existed
bömböge ball
büri (postposed) each, all
    bürin completely, entirely
büriye shell, conch, trumpet
bürkü- to cover, to be covered
bürüi dark, darkness
bütü- to be finished, to conclude
    bütüge- to make, accomplish
büdügün large, heavy
bütün complete, entire

Č

čabči- to cut down, fell; to close
    one's eyes
čabčila- to cut in pieces; to engage
    in sword play

čay time, season
    tere čay-tur at this time, then, thereupon
čayan white
    čayayčin white (fem.)
čayana farther away; behind
čaylaši ügei infinite; peerless
čai (Chin.) tea
čai- to grow light; to bleach, whiten
čambudvib (Skt.) world; Indian continent
čang cymbals
čandali (Skt.) half-caste, low-caste person
čandan|a (Skt.) sandalwood
čaqulai (sea) gull
času|n snow
čadig genealogy
čeberle- to clean
čečeg flower
    čečeglig garden
čengge- to amuse oneself
    čengeldü- to amuse oneself (with others)
čerig (*čirig*) army; soldier; war
čes bronze, brass
či thou, you (2nd. p. sg.) (see § 35)
či = ču
čib|bü- to plunge, submerge, sink
čičuya whip
čiytaya|n gag; cord, string, rope
    čiytayala- to tie up, to gag
čiyul|a- to gather (intr.)
čike right, straight, truthful
čiglen direct
čilayu|n (pl. *-d*) stone
čima- oblique of *či*, thou, you
čime- to adorn, beautify
    čimeg ornaments; attire
čimege|n cry, sound, report
čina- to cook (tr.), prepare (food)
činadu on that side; foreign
    činayši over there; further, behind
činggis qayan Gengis Khan (see Intro.)
čindamani (Skt.) a magical gem
činua (pl. *činus*) wolf
čirai face
čirig (*čerig*) army; soldier; war
čirigle- to wage war
čisu|n blood
čida- to be able; can

čidqu- pour
čoy blaze, splendor, glory
ču (emphatic part.) also, indeed
čuburi- to run, flow (uninterruptedly)
čoyčala- to pile up, to construct
čuyla- to gather, assemble (intr.)
    čuylayul- to collect, assemble (tr.)
čoyol- to make an opening, pierce
čoki- to strike, beat, hammer
čuqay rare, precious
čuqul narrow
čuqum exactly, actually, quite
čöb a bit; remainder
čöble- to pick up grain
čügege- to chase away
čögen few, little
    čögeken some few
čögeresün see *kögesün*
čüle- to banish, exile
čölme- to steal, rustle
čöm all, completely

D see **T**

E

eber horn
ebesü|n (pl. *-d*) grass; plants
ebed- to fall sick, feel bad
ebe(d)či|n sickness
ebde- to destroy, ruin
ebdere- to perish, ruin
ebüge|n old man; grandfather
ebül winter
ebür breast, chest
eče- to grow thin, emaciate
eči- to go
ečige father
    ečige eke parents
ečüs end, goal
eimü so, such, such a one
ein so, such, thus, in this manner
ejen (pl. *ejed*) ruler, master, lord
eke (pl. *-s*) mother
    ekener married woman
egere- to entreat, beg
egešig voice, sound, song
eki|n beginning, source
egüd- to construct, make, manufacture
    arya egüd- to find a way out
egüle|n cloud
    egületü cloudy

egün- oblique form of *ene*
egür- carry on one's back
egüri long
egüs- to begin
egüske- to begin; to produce, make
egüde|n door, entry
elči (pl. *-s, -d*) envoy, ambassador
ele affirmative particle
  ele bögesü if, whatever it be
elegle- to ridicule
elige|n liver, stomach, insides
eljige|n ass, donkey
eldeb all sorts, different, diverse
em medicine, remedy, drug
  emči doctor, physician
eme (pl. *-s*) woman, wife
  emege|n old woman, grandmother
emegel saddle
emiye- to be afraid
emkü morsel, mouthful
emüne before, the place in front of one
  emüne jüg south
emüs- to dress oneself
  emüske- to dress (trans.), to clothe
ene this
enel- to grieve, sorrow
enedkeg India
eng area, space; strengthening particle: the very-, the all-
engke peace, quiet, well-being
enggüre dear, favorite, pet (name)
ende here
  endeče hence, thereupon
  endeki the one here (Ger. hiesige)
ere (pl. *-s*) man, husband
eregün chin
eri- to seek; ask, request
erike|n rosary; chain (of pearls)
erildü- to seek, ask (together); to take counsel
eriyen varicoloured; motley; adorned
erke power, might
  erketen powerful; the senses; the zodiac
ergi- to turn, circle
  ergičegül- to have turned; to think
  ergigü addled, crazy
erkim supreme, chief, outstanding
  erkim aqa good sir!
ergü- to render, present (to a superior)
ermeg barren mare

ersü neuter
erte early, former, ancient
  erte urida once upon a time
erdem talent, merit, virtue, wisdom
erdeni (Skt., pl. *-s*) jewel, treasure
erü- to dig
ese no, not (preposed)
  ese bögesü if it be not so, otherwise, or else, *n'est-ce pas?*
esen safe, well, healthy, prosperous
esergü opposite, against
  esergü tesergü to and fro, hither and yon
esrua (Sogd.) Brahma
ed (Uig.) things, wares, possessions
  ed tavar goods, wealth, fortune
ede- pl. stem of *ene*
edege- recover, heal (intr.)
edegege- heal, restore, revive (tr.)
eteged side, region
edüge now
edüi not yet
edür day
eye peace, accord

G see K

Γ

γayča one, only, sole, alone
  γayčaγar sole, solitary
  γayčaqan only, sole, alone
γai misfortune, evil, injustice
γaiqa- be astonished, surprised; to regard with wonder and admiration
  γaiqaldu- to admire in company
  γaiqamšiγ wonder, marvel; admirable, remarkable
γajar (pl. *γajad*) land, earth, place, country
γal fire
γaljaγu mad, crazy
γaqai pig, swine
γar hand, arm
γar- to come out, go out; to proceed, occur, begin
γarγa- to take out, bring out; to free; to produce
γarta- to be surpassed
γasal- to be afflicted, complain
  γasalang pain, complaint
  γasalulča- to lament in company

γašiγun bitter, harsh
γašiγuda- to be sad, grieve
γadana outside
   γadayši outside
   γadanaši that in front
   γadayur the outside, exterior
γau ditch, crater
   γautu baišing prison
γobi barren steppe, desert, Gobi
γučin thirty
γui- (γuyu-) to ask for, request
γuilinči beggar
γulir meal, ground grain
γurbaγula all three, the three together
γurban three
γorbila- to cover with lime; to bulge
   out (as of relief work)
γutu- to trouble, bother oneself;
   dishonour, lose face
γutaγar third
γutul boot, shoe
γodoli horn-pointed arrow
γooa beautiful, handsome, charming
γool river valley, river; kernel,
   essence; center, origin, source
γuyu (γui-) to ask for, request; to
   ask the hand of

I

ibege- to aid, help, protect
ibegel protection, blessing
ičegüre- to blush with shame, to be
   ashamed
ijaγur root, origin, family clan,
   extraction
ila- to surpass, surmount
   ilaγa- to surmount, overcome
   ilaγaγsan conqueror, majesty
ilege- to send, dispatch (a messenger,
   delegate)
iledte clear, obvious
iledke- to declare, manifest, explain
ilγa- to distinguish, discern, make out
ildü|n sword
ima- oblique stem of 3rd p. sg.
   pronoun (see § 35)
imaγa|n goat, buck
imayta merely, only
inadu on this side; existing, present
   inayši on this side, around here;
   down to the present
   inaru before, until, after

inege- to laugh, smile
inggijü (colloq.) thus, in this way
inje, inji dowry
inu (nom. part., see § 10) indicates
   subject; his
irbis panther, leopard
ire- to come, arrive
   iregül- to make come, to summon,
   invite
irgen persons, people, men
irjailya- to bare one's teeth (at one
   another)
isü|n = yisün nine
ide- to eat
   idegde- to be eaten
   idegen food, repast, meal
   idegül- to give to eat, to feed (tr.)
   idelče- to eat (something) together
   with others
   ideši food, meals
itege- to believe, trust, confide in
idqa- to warn; to stop (tr.), hinder
idqaya warning

J/Y

NB. j/y are identical initially only
-ja emphatic particle; certainly,
   surely
jabsar interval, space, chink
jabdu- to take measures, make pre-
   parations
yabu- to go, walk, travel, wander,
   live
   yabuγul- to make go, to send
   yabulča- to journey together
   yabudal going, conduct, behavior
yayaki- to make what, to do how
   yayakin how?
jaγan elephant
yayara- to hurry
   yayaran hastily
yayuki- to do what, to act how
yayuma object, something
yayu|n what
   yayun ber something
   yayun-dur why, for what (reason)
jaγun hundred
jaγura between, while, during
jaγura- to close together, compress
jaila- to depart, leave; to evade
jaki- to order, command; to proclaim

yaki- to do what, to do how
　yakin why?, how?
jakir- to command, direct, govern
jakirayalayul- to have administer
yakša (Skt.) a Yakṣa, an evil spirit
jala- to summon, invite; to steer
jalayu young; youth
jalbari- to pray, request, implore
jam way, road
yambar which, what kind
jambudvib = čambudvib
jang morals, character, being
jaqa edge, border, bank
yara wound
jarim some, others; half
　jarim-dur sometimes
　jarim . . . jarim some . . . others
jarla- to publish, announce
jarliy word, order, command (of a
　　superior); decree, royal edict
　jarliy bol- to declaim, pronounce;
　　(of a superior) to speak, say,
　　command
jarudasu|n slave, servant, messenger
jasa- to correct, improve, repair; to
　　direct, found, govern
yasu|n bone; lineage
yasutu boned; related
yada- to be unable
yadara- to become exhausted
yadayu poor
jayaya- to bestow (of God), create
　jayayutu having a fate, predestin-
　　ed
jayaya|n will, fate, soul, existence,
　　fortune
yeke large, great, greatness
　yekes (pl.) the great ones (i.e.,
　　gods)
　yekeken rather large
　yekede very, much
jegü- to fasten; to bear; to set a
　　net, snare
yegüdke- to change, move, shift; die
jegüdüle- to dream
　jegüdün a dream
jegü|n needle; left, east
yeren ninety
jerge order, rank, turn
　jergeber in turn
yerü in general, quite; common, usual
　yerünggei general, ordinary; public

jes copper
yi (Chin.) name of a year
jibqulang grandeur, majesty, splen-
　　dour
jiči also, still
jiya- to show, indicate, teach
　jiyala- to be taught
jiyasu|n fish
　jiyasuči|n fisher(man)
jigši- to dislike, hate
jidkü- to be industrious, diligent
jil year
jilvi, jilbi magic, sorcery, deceit
　jilviči|n magician, sorcerer
jilmegül- to show anger
jimis fruit, berries
jiran sixty
jirya- to rejoice, be happy
　jiryalang happiness, prosperity
　jiryayul- to make happy, delight
　jiryaldu- to be happy with others
jiruy painting, picture
　jiruyči painter
jiryuyan six
yirtinčü world
yisün nine
joba- to suffer, sorrow
　jobaya- to make suffer, torment
　jobalang sorrow, suffering, mis-
　　fortune
　jobaldu- to suffer together with
　　others
jočin traveller, guest
joyoyla- to eat and drink, con-
　　sume
joki- to be suitable, satisfactory; to
　　agree with
　jokis excellent, proper; decency
　jokistu proper, conforming to
　　practice
jokiya- to make, fashion, compose
　beleg jokiya- to present, give gifts
jolya- to meet; to visit; to greet
　jolyaldu- to meet one another
juljaya|n young, offspring
juljayala- to give birth to
jum see *gem jum*
jonggila- to collect, assemble
jon people, community
jun summer
jorči- to go away, depart
jurim, jurum law, custom, usage

yosu|n custom, manner, rule
  yosula- to follow custom or usage;
    to observe ceremonies
jöb fine, good, excellent, true
  jöb döröge left stirrup
jöbleldü- to deliberate, confer, hold
    a conference
jöbšiye- to approve, assent
jüil class, type, sort; chapter
jüg side, region, direction; towards
jöge- to move (tr.), transport, carry
jögei insect; bee
jögelen soft, tender, sensitive
yüm = yayuma
jüde- to be exhausted, be disturbed

K / G

ga (Chin.) name of a year
kabalik Kabalik, a city
galab (Skt.) eon, age
garudi (Skt.) a miraculous bird
ge- (colloq.) to say
  ged = geged (Class. *kemeged*)
kebeli stomach, womb
kebte- to lie
gei- to shine, be resplendent
  geigsen the illuminated one
keiske- to wave, scatter, sow, broad-
    cast
  keiste- to be moved; to be driven
    away
keid cloister, monastery
kejiye when, once
  kejiyede sometime, once
(ge)gegen light, bright, illuminated;
    splendour; reincarnation of the
    Buddha, Holy One; person, heart,
    soul
  gegen-degen by one's self; in his
    splendor
  gegen oyutu having a splendid
    intellect, of illuminated con-
    science
geki- to nod assent
kegüken = keüken
kegür corpse, body
kegürjigene pigeon, dove
kele- to say, speak, talk
  kelelče- to converse, discuss to-
    gether
  kele|n tongue, language, speech

gem evil, fault, offense, sin
  gem ügei faultless, just; makes no
    difference
  gem jum fault, mishap, error
keme- to say, speak; to name, call
  kemeldü- to speak to each other
  kemebesü when one says; as if to
    say; for example; because
  kemen saying; equals quotation
    marks
kemkeči- break, crush
gemle- to harbor a grudge, be mal-
    content
gemšigülengtü repentant, contrite
ken (pl. *ked*) who, which
  kenü whose
  ken ber someone
  ken kümün any man, anyone
genedte suddenly, all at once
kengerge drum
ger (pl. *-üd*) tent, home, house; family
ker how
  ker be if
  ker bolba actually
  ker büri everyone
keregür quarrel
kereg necessity; matter, thing, affair
  keregle- to need, require; to
    demand, use
  keregtü necessary, needed
kerem mound, wall
gergei wife
  gergei bolulča- to marry
kešig favor, good luck, fortune, grace
gešigün branch, member, part
ged from *ge-*
gedergü back, behind
getül- to traverse, pass, cross
kedü|n how many; some, few
  arban kedün some ten, ten-odd
  kedüdüger which, how many
  kedünde how many times
ketürkei distinguished, superior,
    excellent
keüken (pl. *keüked*) child
gi (Chin.) name of a year
ki- to make, fashion, construct,
    arrange
  kiged and, also, together
kičiye- to strive, work at, apply
    oneself
gički- to step, trample

kijayar border, edge, end, shore, bank
kigiri banner, guidon
kilyasu|n hair
kilinča sin, fault
kilingle- to become angry
gilte splendour
kimura- to be troubled, be disorderly
kimusu|n claws
ginji chains, fetters
ging (Chin.) name of a year
kirtü- to get dirty, soiled
kidu- to cut, kill
  kituya knife
kkib (kiib) a silken cloth
kšan (Skt.) moment, instant
goršiša (Tib.) a type of sandalwood
kü strengthening part. (see § 51b)
köbči bowstring; chain; mountain ridge
gübčin all, entire
köbege edge, border, bank
köbegün (pl. -d) son; young man
küčü|n power, strength
  küčütü (-tei) strong, powerful
güi (Chin.) name of a year
güiče- to finish, end, complete
küji perfume, incense
küjügü|n neck
kög sound, voice, music
köke blue; green
  kökere- to become blue
köge- to hunt, pursue
  kögelge- to have driven away
kögerükü poor (man)!
kögesün čögeresün scum, foam
gügi- to fish with hook and line
köl foot, leg; basis, action
költü tailed
kölemji, kölümji cave, lair
küliye- to wait for
kölge|n mount; means of transport, wagon
kölgele- to ride horseback
kümün human, man
gün deep, depth; dark
künesü|n provisions
künjid sesame
könggen easy, easy, light
köndeile- to hollow out
köndelen across, on the side

kündü weight, weighty, important; value
kündüle- to show respect
kündülel honour, respect
könüge- to injure, mistreat
kür- to come, arrive, attain, reach; grow to
körbe- to topple over, tumble; to roll on the ground
kürčemtü distinguished, illustrious
küriye|n camp, enclosure, compound
  küriyele- to pitch camp, make a ring
  küriyelegül to become encircled, surrounded
kürge- to bring, have come, lead
köröngge grain, seed
kürte- to attain, reach, get
  kürtege- to have someone get; to honour with a favour
kürtele going as far as, until
körüg picture, painting
kürügül- to bring; to send
görügesün wild game
küse- to desire, covet, wish
  küsel wish, desire
köser earth, soil, ground
köšigürke- to be stubborn
košigürken ögüle- to contradict, dispute
ködege open steppe, desert
kötel-, kötöl- to lead, conduct; to move
kötelül movement

L

lab really, exactly, truly
labai sea shell; mother of pearl
lama see blama
lang (Chin.) ounce of silver, a taël
luu (Chin.?) dragon

M

mayad certainly; really
mayta- praise, laud
mayu evil, bad, poor, unhappy
  mayu bol- to get hurt, injured
  mayušiya- to blame, reproach
mal livestock, cattle
malta- to dig
man- oblique stem of ba, we (see § 35)

mana- to hold night watch; to make the rounds as guard

manaγar next day

maryada morning; tomorrow

mariya- to steal up on, creep up stealthily

maši many, much, very

mašida very, extremely

matar sea monster

matar jögei crocodile

meküiski- to bow respectfully, to greet

meküs weak, exhausted, poor

melekei, menekei frog, toad, turtle

m(e)ngdeni- to be disturbed, upset

mendü, mengdü healthy, whole

mergen clever, wise, capable

mede- to know, learn, experience

medegül- to make known, inform

metü (pl. *metüs*) postposed; as, like, similar

mingyan thousand

minu my

miqa|n meat, flesh; body

moγai (pl. *moγas*) snake, serpent

molor = *bolor*

mongγol (pl. *-čud*) Mongol, Mongolian

mungla- to be in need

mungdal ügei extraordinarily, abundantly

mungdani- to be in need

mungqaγ ignorance

morila- to ride horseback, mount to horse

mori|n (pl. *-d*) horse

moritu having a horse; a rider

morda- to set out, depart (on horseback)

modu|n wood, tree, forest

modući woodworker, carpenter, joiner

muski- twist, wind

munu- to weaken, age

möltöre- to loosen, detach, release; to escape

mön deictic particle: just that one; certainly, surely, really

mön kü just that one there; the same

mönggü|n silver; money

möngke eternal, everlasting

mör way, road, track, order, row, method

tere mör-iyer along that road

mören (pl. *möred*) river, stream

mörgö- to bow respectfully; to kow-tow

mörö|n shoulder

möski- to follow a track, to trail

mösün ice

N

nabtarqai ragged

naγad- to play, amuse oneself

naγaču uncle (on mother's side)

naγadum game, amusement

naγur lake, sea

naičiγar fat

naiman eight

naira- to agree; to unite

nairaγul- to reconcile, bring to accord; mix (colours, drugs)

nairala- to celebrate, amuse oneself

nairalčin soft; foolish

nairamdaγu agreed, united

nama- oblique of *bi,* I (see § 35)

nara|n sun

narin thin, slender; secret

nasu|n age, years of life

nasula- to attain an age

nasun turqaru forever, always

nasuda entire life, unceasingly

nadur see § 35

nayan eighty

nege- to open

negüresü|n charcoal, coal

neng much, very

n(e)ngji investigation, search

nere name, title

neretü named

nereid- to name, call

niγu- to hide, secrete

niγuča secret

niγur face

nige|n a, one

nigeken only one, a single

nijeged one at a time, one each

edür-ün nijeged once a day

nigül sin

nigüles- to commiserate, sympathize

nigülesügči merciful one

nigültü sinful, sinner

nilbusu|n tear
nilqa|n (pl. *-s*) child
nirvan (Skt.) Nirvāna, release of the soul from suffering, union with the absolute
nis- to fly
nisvanis (Skt.) attachment to the world; inherent evil
nitula- to kill
nidü|n eye
nidügür pestle
noγoγan green; plants
noγon boy
noir sleep
noitan fresh, moist
nom (ult. < Greek) doctrine, belief, dharma; book; duty, obligation
   nomčila- to teach, instruct
   nomla- to teach, instruct
noqai dog
noyan (pl. *noyad*) prince, nobleman, ruler
   noyalaγči tyrant
nögči- to pass (of time); to end, die
nökör (pl. *nököd*) comrade, friend, companion
   nököče- to ally oneself with, make friends
nögöge second, other

O see U

Ö see Ü.

Q

qabčil ravine, pass
qabiya benefit, profit
qabtayai flat
qabur spring
qačar cheek, jaw
qaγa- to close, lock
qaγača- to be separated, removed; to depart
   qaγačaγul- to remove, deprive of
qaγalγa|n gate, door, entrance; Kalgan
qaγal- to cut; to plow
qaγa quite, apart
qaγara- to crack, split
qaγan emperor, king, Khan
qaγas half
qaγučin old, ancient
   qaγučin üge proverb

qayurayda- to be deceived
qayurai dry
qayuryal heap, pile, ditch
qaira mercy, grace, sympathy, pity
   qairan bainam that is a pity
   qairala- to love, show mercy; take pity
   qairatai beloved
qairčay chest, casket
qaja- to bite
qajir griffon; vulture
qalayun heat, warmth
   qalayuča- to be warm, feverish
qali- to fly, take off; die
qamiya where, whither
   qamiyaši whither
qamtu (postposed) together with
   qamtuda in union with, jointly
qamuy all, every; quite complete
qan (pl. *qad*) prince, lesser ruler
   qan köbegün prince
   qan oron throne; capital
qan- to be satisfied
   qangya- to satisfy
   qaniča- to be a friend of, be related to
   qanila- to contract friendship
qandu- to turn
   qanduyul- to turn (tr.), direct
   qanuši ügei dissatisfied, malcontent; incapable of satisfying
qara black
qara- to see, regard, notice
   qarabtur dark, pitch-black
   qarayalja- to see, observe
   qarayda- to show oneself, be seen
qarayul sentinel, guard
   qarayul- to make see; to watch (herd)
   qarayulči guard; shepherd
qarai- to spring, leap (down, into)
   qaraila- to spring high, leap up
qarangyui dark, darkness; ignorance; hell
qarbisu|n womb, belly
qarbu- to shoot with bow and arrow
qarčayai hawk, falcon
qari- to return (home)
   qarin again, but
qariyu back, return, reply, reward
   qariyul- to return (tr.); to reward; to answer
qarilčan together, mutual, reciprocal

qariya dependence, subject
qariyatu subordinate, subject, vassal
qarkitu running (water)
qarši court, palace, castle
qas jasper, jade
qašira- to become tired, bored
qatayu solid, tough, cruel, hard
qadayala- to keep, watch
  qadayalayul- to have kept, watched
qada|n rock, cliff
qatayuji- to do penance
qataqan rather strong, hard; quite certain, self-confident
qadqu- to stick; to plant
qatuytai woman, wife
qadum male in-law
  qadum ečige father-in-law
qatun queen, princess, wife, woman
qauli custom, tradition; saga, story
qubaqai dried up, parched
qubčasu|n garments, clothing
qubi part, piece
  qubi bolya- to divide
qubil- to transform oneself
  qubilya- to transform (tr.)
  qubilyan transformation, shape; reincarnation
qočora- to remain, be left over
quyu (breaking) in two, apart
qoyola|i throat; food
quyur lute, balalaika
quyurda- to play on the *quyur*
quyura- to break
quyurqai piece, torn off portion
qoyosun absence, lack, empty space
qoiy island
qoina after, later, since
  qoinayši|da after, behind
qoitu behind, rear; the future
qokira- to wither
qola far, distant
qulayaiči thief
qulayu- to steal
qula|n roan and white horse
qoli- to mix
quluyana mouse
qumay, qumaki sand
qomsa small, insignificant
  qomsad- to diminish, decrease (intr.)

qongqo bell
qongqor depth, cavern; chestnut horse
qoni|n (pl. -*d*) sheep
qono- to live, dwell (overnight)
  qonoy 24-hour period, a day and night
qoor|a evil, poison
  qoortu evil, poisonous
  qoor bol- to be hard on, bad for
  qoorla- to harm, poison
qura rain
qura- to assemble, gather (intr.)
  qural assembly
qorya castle, fort
qurya|n lamb
qori- to collect, press; to mix, blend
qoriča- to desire; to love
qoriyla- to reprimand, swear at
qorim, qurim feast, banquet, celebration
  qorimla- to celebrate, feast
qurimqan = qurum
qorin twenty
quriya- to collect, gather, assemble
qormusu|n silken gauze
qurdun agile, swift
qoroya- to reduce; to kill
quruyu|n finger
qoroqai insects, worms, vermin, etc.
qoros- to become angry, offended
qorum, qurum moment, instant
qorumqan = qorum
qos pair, couple
quda brother-in-law; cousin
qudal deceit, lie
qudaldu- to sell, deal in
  qudalduyan trade, commerce
  qudalduyči dealer, merchant
  qudaldu|n trade
qota|n fortress; city, town
quduy well
qutuy dignity, distinction; divinity, holiness
  qutuy yuyu- to pray
  qutuytu elevated, venerable, saintly; a title
qotola, qotala all, every
qudurya tail strap
quvaray (Uig.) community of clergy
quyay armor

qoyar two; and
qoyaduyar second
qoyayulaqan-a two all by themselves
qoyar büri both of them

R

rasba (Tib.) person wearing cotton clothes; an Indian ascetic

S

saba container
sača at once, immediately
sačayu equal, similar; at the same time as
saču- to strew, sow, disperse
sadu|n close friend
sayad delay, difficulty
sayatayul- to delay, defer, prolong
sayu- to sit, be seated, live, dwell
sayulya- to set, place, appoint
saiki proper name?
sain good, fine
saiqan beautiful, pretty
saišiya- to approve, praise, reward
saitur good, well, very; (will you) kindly
saki- to watch, protect
sakiyulsu|n watcher, defender; patron saint
salkin wind
salu- to depart, separate (oneself)
sana- to think, recall, remember
sanaya thought, idea, memory
sanal thought, memory
sang (Chin.) treasure, treasury
sandali throne, chair
saqal beard
sara|n month; moon
sarqud intoxicating beverages, wine
seilü- to carve, engrave
sejig = sešig
sejigle- to doubt, distrust
segsei- to bristle, raise
segül tail, end
següder shadow
selte (postposed) together with; party company
sem silence, silently
serbege notch, hook; gills, fins

sergü- to come to oneself, regain senses
sergüge- to cheer up, console
seri- to awake, wake
serigül- to wake; to teach
serigün cool, refreshing, pleasant
sešig (Uig.) doubt, disbelief
sedki- to think, consider
sedkil thought, intent, purpose; mind
sedkiltü disposed
sedkiši ügei unthinkable
sedkül courier, journal
sedkügül- to dispatch as courier
sedü- to make, accomplish
arya sedü- to employ means
si- see *ši-*
sin (Chin.) name of a year
subašidi (Skt.) Subhāṣita
suburya|n pagoda, memorial
soči- to become frightened
soyta- to get drunk
soytaya- to drink until drunk
sumu|n arrow
sonos- to hear, listen
sonosta- to be reported, be heard
sonosqa- to make known, inform
sonosqayul- to have announce, have report
soqora- to become blind
sur- to learn, study; to ask
surya- to instruct, teach
soyoya eyeteeth
soyorqa- to deign; will you please ...; to present
sübei opening, passage
süke|n ax
sülde happiness; protector gods; banner; totem
sü|n milk
sünesün life's breath, soul; the soul of personal mannerisms and actions
söni night
sürči- to grease, oil, perfume
sür(e)kei terrifying

Š

šal (onomat.) splash
šang reward
šangna- to reward

šarya bay-colored
  šaryuyul a white and red horse
šastir (Skt.) a sāstra; learned work, textbook, commentary
šibayu|n bird
  šibayuči bird catcher
šibar dirt, mud, clay
šibegčin slave, servant
šibtura- to pierce (of arrows);
šiyu- to tuck one's clothes up
šijir pure gold; advantage
šikür canopy, parasol
silyad- to tremble
šiltayan cause, reason
šiluyu|n straight, simple, loyal
  šiluyunqan quite direct, straight-forward
šim (Chin.) name of a year
šim a measure (ten double handfuls)
šimgü- to steal into, crawl up to
šimda- to hasten; strive, work at
šinbi- to get into a mess
šine new
šinggi (colloq.) same, as, like
šingšiči fortune teller
šingqor falcon
šinjile- to regard, observe; investigate
šinu- to desire, covet; to require
šiqa- to press, express; approach
šira yellow
širayu- to seek refuge
širege|n table, throne, chair, dais
širgüge- to rub against, provoke
širge dried, cooked
širya see *šarya*
širi|n hide, skin, leather
širyu- to creep, crawl
široi earth, soil
šitaya- to ignite
šidi (Skt.) completeness, perfection
šidi(n)tü kegür Siddhi Kür, the Bewitched Corpse
šiduryu simple, right, just
šitü- to support; to join, go in service to
šidü|n tooth

T /D

ta you
da emph. part., *ken da* someone

daba- to cross over; to transgress
dabayan mountain; pass
dabalya|n wave
tabčang throne, plateau
tabin fifty
dabqur double
  dabqurliy doubling, multiplication
tabtayar fifth
tabun five
tačiya- to desire ardently, love passionately
  tačiyangyui passion, sensual love; desire
daya- to accompany, follow, obey
dayan following; also
dayayul- to have follow; to make obey
tayala- to want, desire; love, find pleasure in
  tayalal love, pleasure, wish
dayari- to pass, meet
  dayariju gar- to pass
dayu|n voice, sound, song
  dayula- to sing
  dayun yar- to cry out
  dayuda- to invite, summon
dayuriya- to imitate
dayuris- to become renowned
  dayurisqa- to voice, proclaim
dayus- to end, finish
tail- to open, loosen (clothes), free
daila- to combat
  dailalda- to vie with one another
dain enemy
daisun enemy
taki- to sacrifice; worship;
daki again, also
daki- repeat
takil respect, worship
dakin again
takiya poultry, chicken
tala steppe, plain, field
tala- to capture
dalabči|n wing; tailfeather
dalai sea, ocean
dalan seventy
talbi- to put, place; to release, leave
  talbiyul- to set, have placed
dalda hidden, secret
dam dam from one to the other
tamaya seal, stamp

tamaki tobacco
  tamaki uyu- to smoke
tamir strength, power
tamu (Skt.) hell
dan very, quite, often
tan- oblique stem of *ta*
tangyariy oath, vow
  tangyariyla- to swear, vow
tangqai coarse, impolite; simple,
    ordinary
tani- to know, learn
  tanildu- to meet, get to know
taraki, tariki brains, head
tarbayačila- to trap marmots
darbayulya flag, banner
dargi trunk
tariy see *uruy tariy*
tariya|n field
  tariyači farmer, field worker
tarni (Skt., pl. *-s*) magical formula
  tarnida- to recite magical formulæ
tarqa- to disperse, go (each his own
    way)
  tarqaya- to make disperse; to
    promulgate, publish
daru- to press, repress, conquer; to
    print
  daruyda- to be pressed, printed
darui immediately, straightway;
    moment
tasu perfectivizing particle
tasu- to be accustomed to
tasul- to interrupt, separate, finish
  tasural division, interruption
tata- to pull, draw, tighten
taulai hare
tavar (Uig.) goods, effects, belongings
  ed tavar possessions
tebči- to release, abandon; to slay
debel = *degel*
teberildü- to embrace each other
debši- to climb, mount
  debšigül- to raise, advance (tr.),
    promote
debter book
deile- to defeat, surpass
teimü so, such, such a, thus
tein so thus
  tein bögesü if, for this reason, then
tejiye then, long ago
  tejiyede then, at that time, once
tejiye- to rear, bring up

degedü high, elevated, noble
  degegši upwards
degel cloak, coat; clothes
degere upper, above, overhead
  degereki the one over, above
degerme robber, robbery
degesü|n rope, cord
tegü- to gather, pick
degü younger brother
tegülder perfect, complete
tegüli- to spring, bound
tegün- oblique of *tere*
  tegünčilen thus, in this manner, so
tegüs perfect, complete
  tegüs- to perfect, fulfill, complete
tel quryan suckling lamb
del mane
deled- to strike, beat
  deledkile- to knock, rattle
delgere- to develop, expand
  delgerenggüi development, exposi-
    tion
  delgerenggui-e detailedly
delekei earth, world
delüre- to come to oneself
temeči- to quarrel, dispute; compete
temege|n camel
temür iron
teneg stupid, foolish
tenggerlig gods, heaven
tengri heaven; god
  tengri bol- to die
tengse- to compare, examine
  tengsel comparison, examination
tende there
  tendeče thence, thereupon, then
  tendeki the one there (Ger. dortige)
tere that, that one, he
terge chariot, wagon
tergegür highway
dergede before, by, beside, at, *chez*
terigü|n head; beginning; first
  terigüle- to begin; to be chief
  terigülen et al., etc., and others
  terigüten first, principal; *et al.*
tes- to suffer, endure, hold out
  teske- to make suffer, let endure
  tesül- to gouge out eyes
tede- plural oblique of *tere*
tedeger pl. of *tere*, strengthened
tedüi so much, up to; after, there-
    upon

ding (Chin.) name of a year
tngri = tengri
tobčayan history, account
tobči button; summary, resume
tobray dust, ground
dobtul- to pursue, attack
tuy banner
toya number, amount
  toya tomši ügei since time im-
    memorial
  toyatan numbered, counted
toyo- to count, calculate
  toyoči mathematician
  toyola- to calculate, consider
toyol- to pass through; to become
    perfect
duyul- to comprehend
tuyura(i) hoof
duyuriy circle
toyori- to go around, revolve
  toyoriyul- to make turn, revolve (tr.)
toyos peacock
toyosqa brick, tile
toytaya- to stop; to appoint, establish
toin monk
doki- to bow one's head
tokiya- to merit, deserve; to act in
    unison
tul- to attain, reach
tula (postposed) for, on account of,
    because of, in order to
tulada = tula
dolgi|n wave
doliya- to lick
toli|n mirror
toloyai head, peak, beginning
doloyan seven
doloyoyna a red thirst-quenching
    berry
doluya- to lick
tomši see *toya tomši ügei*
dumda middle, center
  dumda oron middle land, central
    India: China
  dumdadu middle, central
  dumdaki the one in the middle
dongyod- to cry, scream
tungyay announcement, declaration
tonil- to be saved
  tonilya- to save
toor net,
doora under, down, lower

ene doora here (under this place)
  dooraki the one under
tuqai circumstance, time, manner,
    means
dura|n desire, wish, inclination
  durala- to desire, wish
durad- to remember, think about,
    converse
torya|n silk
doroyši downwards
doroida- to weaken (intr.), be con-
    quered
  doroidayul- to weaken (tr.), con-
    quer
doromjila- to humiliate, insult
turqaru in *nasun turqaru*, all one's life
tus against, before
  tus bol- to occur, happen; to show
    up, come upon
  tus tus-tur each for himself
tusa usefulness, aid, advantage
  ači tusa reward
  tusala- to aid, help, serve
toso- to support; bar
  toson ab- to catch, trap
dusu- to flow, drip
tosu|n oil, grease, butter
tušiya- to hand over, give, deliver
tušiya|n chains, fetters
duta- to lack
  dutaya- to cause to lack; to take
    flight, flee
dotoyla- to prefer
dotoyši inside, in
dotora inside, in, the inner
  dotorki the one inside
todorqai clear, distinct
todqur obstacle, evil, misfortune
tutum each, all
duvaja (Skt.) banner
döčin forty
tüidker hindrance, obstacle
töge span
tügeile- to suspect
tügemel all, in general, completely
dügür- to fill up, fulfill
  dügüreng full
tögörig Mongolian monetary unit
tüle- to burn, set fire to
  tülegde- to be burned
  tüliye firewood
tülkigür key

6 Grønbech

tümen ten thousand
tün forest, grove, cave
tüne|n dark
dörbel obstacle
dörbeljin square, quadratic (script)
dörben four
türgen quick
düri form, shape, nature
dürsü|n form, shape, object
törö law, custom, usage, government
dürü- to insert, place in
törö- to be born, to arise
döröge stirrup
töröl birth, race, parentage
tüšimel (pl. *tüšimed*) official, minister
dötöger fourth

0 /U

u (Chin.) name of a year
u interr. part., see § 44 c
oboyala- to pile up
oboy clan, family, generation
učir reason, cause; content, circumstances
učira- to meet; to coincide
  učiraldu- to meet each other; to be in touch with
uya- to wash
oytal- to cut up, slaughter; to cut down
oytaryui heaven, sky
uytu- to meet
  uytuyul- to send to meet
uyu- to drink
  uyulya- to give to drink
  uyuči swallow, gulp
uyuta sack, bag
oi wood, forest, park
uil whirlpool, whirlwind
uila- to weep
oira near, close
oirata- to approach, to near
oiratu- to approach
uidqar melancholy, affliction
okila- to cry, lament
ugiya- to wash oneself
ol- to find, acquire, obtain
ulayan red
olayula many at a time
ulam gradually, bit by bit
  ulam-iyar gradually, by degrees
ulamjila- to do progressively; to say to someone by means of another

olan very, many
ulari- to change, replace, move (tr.)
olboya track (in the grass)
olda- to be found, acquire
olong saddle girth
ulus nation, people, state
umai womb
umara north
umarta- to forget
ombo- to swim
omo milk
omoy = *oboy*
omoy pride, arrogance
  omoyla- to be proud
umdayan drink, beverage
umdayas- to be thirsty
umta- to sleep
on (pl. *od*) year
una- to fall, fall down
onča only, sole
oni notch in arrow; mountain pass
  onila- to set arrow to bow
onisu|n lock, spring; interior, essence
ungyasu|n wool
ongyoča ship
ongyon pure, sacred; the spirit inhabiting a material object
ungši- to read
unji- to hang
unta- to sleep
unu- to ride horseback
  unuyul- to help to horse
  unulya beast of burden, riding animal
uqa- to understand
  uqaya|n reason, intellect
  uqayatu possessed of reason, intelligent
uqu- to dig, hollow out
urala- to use craft, wiles
uran art, craft; handworker, artisan
uraqa bird trap
urba- to turn about; move, change
orči- to turn, revolve
  orčin around, about
  orčilang revolution; existence, organic world of beings
urida before, previously, once
  uridqan-a a little ahead, in front of
  uridu previous, former
  uridučilan as before, in the old way
urin anger, passion

oriyaldu- to intertwine
uri- to call, invite
orki- to throw; a perfectivizing
auxiliary, to finish
oro- to enter
qura oro- to rain
oroγul- to make enter, introduce
oroi top, summit
naran oroi bol- day breaks, dawns
örlüge oroi čai- day breaks, dawns
oron place, land; kingdom, state;
instance, circumstance
oros Russian
oroši- to enter, dwell, approach
orošiγul- to introduce; to bring
about
orošil entrance, introduction
urtu long
ordu palace; camp, horde
oro place, bed
uruγ tariγ family and friends
uruγu below, beneath
urus- flow
usnir headband, topknot
usu|n water
usutu watery
usula- to water (horses)
od- to go, proceed
uda- to linger, dwell; to pass (of
time)
otači doctor, physician
udaγa time, opportunity
utaγa|n smoke
odo = edüge
odolča- to accompany
odqan youngest
odu|n star
udurid- to lead, go in front, show
the way
uduridqa- to have show the way,
to guide, teach
uduriduγči leader, guide, teacher
uya- to bind, tie
uyara- to make soft, relax
oyun reason, intellect, soul, heart
oyutu intelligent, reasonable

Ö /Ü

öbči- to skin
öber oneself
öbere different, other, strange
öbere, öbere each for himself

öberid- to watch as one's own
öber-iyen oneself
öbesüben oneself
öbür = ebür
öči- to say, answer (respectfully)
üčügen small, young
üčügüken minor, a very little
üile deed, work, action, use
üiled- to make, do, create, carry
out
üje- to see, observe; read, study;
visit
üjegde- to show oneself, appear,
seem
üjegül- to show, teach
üjesküleng appearance; handsome,
beautiful; a beauty
üjügür end, tip, point
ög- to give; see also § 54
üge (pl. *üges*) word, speech, saying
qayučin üge proverb
ügei (postposed) without, absence,
lack, no sort of
ügei bol- to die
ükeger corpse, cemetery, grave
ügegü poor; not existing
ügeküre- to become poor
ügegüye both ... and; not
üker (pl. *üked*) cattle, livestock
ögere = öbere
ögeši|n net for birds, fish
ögede upwards
ögede bol- to arise, come, appear
ögedele- to arise, mount
ökin (pl. *ökid*) girl, daughter
ögire- to wither, decay
öglige alms
ükü- to die
ükügül- to kill
ükül death
üküleng death
üküdel corpse
ögügül- to have give
ögül = ebül
ögüle- to say, speak, talk, tell
ögülegde- to be said
ögülel word, statement; verb
ögüleldü- to talk together, say to
one another
üküdkü- to faint
ügürge load, burden, cargo
öl food, provisions

80 Glossary

üle- to remain, be left over; to surpass

ülemji more, greater, superior; chiefly

üliger story, history; comparison, model

üliger-ün dalai The Sea of Stories

öljei happiness

ölögčin female animal

ölöng famine; meadow

ölös- to hunger

ülde- to hunt, pursue

üldegde- to be hunted, driven away

ülü (preposed) no, not

ömgeri- to turn, roll, twist

ömkü- to put in one's mouth, to chew

ünege|n fox

ünemši- to believe, trust, recognize the truth

üne|n true, truth

üneger certainly, indeed

üne|n price, value

ünetü valuable

ünesü|n ash

öngge colour

önggüi- to stick out one's head

öni long ago

üniye|n cow

öndür high

ör dawn

örlüge early

üre fruit, seed, descendant; consequences, profit, advantage, reward

üre- to lose oneself, disappear, escape

üreji- to increase

örgege residence of a prince

örgen wide, width

örgesün thorn

ürgülji always, incessant

ürgüljide unremittingly

örlüge early

ös- to grow up

öske- to bring up, rear

öskilge kick

üsü|n hair

ösür- to rush forward; to sprinkle, splash

öšiye hate, animosity

öd ügei vain, useless

ödter quickly

ötel- to age

üde noon

üde- to lead, accompany

üdeši evening

ödü|n feather

üye member, part; age, time; generation

üye qoyar both together

üyer flood

V

vačir, včir (Skt.) thunderbolt; diamond

vaiduriya (Skt.) lapis lazuli

Y see **J**

Index of Formatives

Front vowels: *e, i, ö, ü*; (require *k /g*)
Back vowels: *a, i, o, u*; (require *q /γ*)

-güjei, timative imperative, § 47 e
-gesei, optative, § 47 d
-gül-, causative, § 41
-güle, forms collective numbers, § 46 c
-γa-, causative, § 41
-γa, continuative verbal noun, § 39 b
-γad, coordinative gerund, § 26
-γan, reflexive suffix used after vowels in genitive, ablative, comitative, § 20
-γasai, optative, § 47 d
-γči, present participle, § 30 b
-γčin, adjectival suffix, denoting feminine, § 22
-γda-, medio-passive, after vowels, § 42
-γdaqui, passive infinitive, used as polite imperative, § 47 f
-γsaγar, < *-γsan* + *bar*, instrumental of preterite participle, § 31 c
-γsan, preterite participle, § 30 c
-γtun, polite imperative, § 47 a
-γujai, timative imperative, § 47 e
-γul-, causative, § 41
-γula, forms collective numbers, § 46 c
-i, accusative, consonant stems, § 12
-iyan, reflexive suffix used after consonants, in genitive-accusative, dative, instrumental, § 20
-iyar, instrumental, after consonants, § 16
-iyar-iyan, instrumental, reflexive, § 20
-iyen, reflexive suffix used after consonants, in genitive-accusative, dative, instrumental, § 20
-iyer, instrumental, after consonants, § 16
-iyer-iyen, instrumental, reflexive, § 20
-ju, subordinating gerund, after vowels and *-l*, § 29 b
-juqui, past tense form, see § 33 b
-jü, subordinating gerund, after vowels and *-l*, § 29 b
-jüküi, past tense form, see § 33 b
-ke, causative suffix, § 41
-kei, pronominal suffix, § 35
-ken, strengthening suffix, § 52 d
-ki, suffix to case forms, making a noun, § 52 c

-kü(i), infinitive (also called future participle), § 30 a
-l, noun, derived from verb, § 39 c
-la-, forms verbs from nouns, § 53
-lang, nominal suffix, § 55
-le-, forms verbs from nouns, § 53
-lča-, reciprocal voice, § 43
-lče-, reciprocal voice, § 43
-ldu-, reciprocal voice, § 43
-ldü-, reciprocal voice, § 43
-leng, nominal suffix, § 55
-lge-, causative voice, § 41
-lγa-, causative voice, § 41
-luγa, perfect tense, § 33 a
-luγa, comitative case, § 17
-luγa-ban, comitative, reflexive, § 20
-lüge, perfect tense, § 33 a
-lüge, comitative case, § 17
-lüge-ben, comitative, reflexive, § 20
-m, durative, alternate form to *-mui*, § 26
-mui, durative, § 26
-müi, durative, § 26
-n₂ gerund of absolute subordination, § 29 a
-n, stem consonant, stable or variable, see § 18
-nar- plural suffix, § 24 a
-ner- plural suffix, § 24 a
-nuγud, plural suffix, § 24 e
-nügüd, plural suffix, § 24 e
-qa, causative suffix, § 41
-qai, pronominal suffix, § 35
-qan, strengthening suffix, § 52 d
-qu(i), infinitive (also called future participle), § 30 a
-ra, forms verbs from nouns, § 53
-ra, gerund of purpose, § 34 b
-re, forms verbs from nouns, § 53
-re, gerund of purpose, § 34 b
-run, gerund of reporting, § 34 a
-rün, gerund of reporting, § 34 a
-s, plural suffix, vowel stems, § 24 c
-su, intentional imperative (older form), § 47 b
-suγai, intentional imperative, § 47 b
-sun, nominal ending, dropped in plural, § 24 d, § 55
-sü, intentional imperative (older form), § 47 b
-sügei, intentional imperative, § 47 b

-*sün*, nominal ending, dropped in plural, § 24 d, § 55
-*ši*, nominal ending, § 55
-*šiya-*, forms verbs from nouns, § 53
-*šiye-*, forms verbs from nouns, § 53
-*tai*, modern comitative, § 22
-*tayan*, dative, reflexive, § 20
-*tai*, adjectival suffix (old feminine form), § 22
-*taki*, nominal suffix 'the one in (a thing)', § 52 c
-*tala*, terminative gerund, § 34 d
-*tan*, adjectival suffix, plural, § 22
-*tegen*, dative, reflexive, § 20
-*tei*, modern comitative, § 22
-*tei*, adjectival suffix (old feminine form), § 22
-*teki*, nominal suffix 'the one in (a thing)', § 52 c
-*tele*, terminative gerund, § 34 d
-*ten*, adjectival suffix, plural, § 22
-*tu*, modern dative, § 14
-*tu*, adjectival suffix, § 22
-*tuyai*, optative imperative, § 47 d
-*tur* dative, § 14
-*tur-iyan*, dative, reflexive, § 20
-*tü*, modern dative, § 14
-*tü*, adjectival suffix, § 22
-*tügei*, optative imperative § 47 d
-*tür-iyen*, dative, reflexive, § 20
-*tür*, dative, § 14
-*u-*, vowel intercalated before suffix beginning with consonant, § 25

-*u*, genitive, after -*n*, § 11
-*ud*, plural suffix, § 24 d
-*un*, genitive, consonant stems, § 11
-*ü-*, vowel intercalated before suffix beginning with consonant, § 25
-*ü*, genitive, after -*n*, § 11
-*üd*, plural suffix, § 24 d
-*ün*, genitive, consonant stems, § 11
-*y-*, form of *i* between vowels
-*y-*, consonant preceding suffix beginning with vowel, used after vowel stems, cf. §§ 11, 12
-*ya*, voluntative imperative, § 47 c
-*ya*, continuative noun, § 39 b
-*ya-*, causative suffix after -*i*, § 41
-*ye*, voluntative imperative, § 47 c
-*ye*, continuative noun, § 39 b
-*ye-*, causative suffix, after -*i*, § 41
-*yi*, accusative, vowel stems, § 12
-*yin*, genitive, vowel stems, § 11
-*yu*, verbal form, see § 33 c
-*yuban*, reflexive form of genitive & accusative, § 20
-*yuyan*, reflexive form of genitive & accusative, § 20
-*yü*, verbal form, see § 33 c
-*yüben*, reflexive form of genitive & accusative, § 20
-*yügen*, reflexive form of genitive & accusative, § 20
- -, (zero ending) simple imperative, § 47 a

SUPPLEMENTS

By John R. Krueger

Supplement to the Grammar

§ 2—a. The question of how to pronounce Classical Mongolian is not an easy one, and it is resolved by the Mongols themselves in various ways. Most persons pronounce a written text more or less as they would speak their own speech, just as an Englishman reading aloud an American novel will use his own accent. Some Mongols use a style that follows the script conventions closely (a sort of spoken *oratio plena*), others convert the script entirely to a modern speech style (in effect almost re-translating it to their dialect), and still others create a blend of the text and their speech which may vary slightly at each reading. My recommendation is for foreign students of Classical Mongolian to pronounce it artificially, with a European-style value of vowels and consonants, as it is spelled, because this will be better for them when they are reading text in native script. At a later time, should they master the popular speech, they can easily convert their literal reading style to a modern spoken style. Final voiced consonants may be pronounced unvoiced at the end of a word or syllable.

§ 2—b. Although there is no notation in vertical script for long vowels, the long vowels are there nonetheless, as in such words as *kemēkü, baiyā*, or endings as *-bāsu, -āča*. This shows up clearly when old script texts are cited today in Cyrillic Mongolian in modern books.

If $s + i$ occurs across a morpheme boundary, there is no resultant *š* (e.g., *üge*, word, *üges*, words, *üges-i*, words, accusative).

§ 10. The nominative particles, to which number we can add *bolbasu* 'if it be', *kemebesü* 'if one say', and *üǰebesü* 'if one consider', function as markers to set off a topic phrase, almost disjunctively. The phrase "as for" (cf. Jap. *wa*) is often a good way to translate such a particle. Since the nominative particle sets off a phrase, it may sometimes occur after a case ending, as in these examples.

SK 38b10	*tere bičig-dür inu*	As for (what was) in this letter
UD 19a4	*busud töröl-dür ber*	As for (what he had done) in other rebirths
SK 3b4	*tedeger-dür ber*	As for (what was) at them, as for what they had
SK 8a7	*arγa-i ber*	As for the scheme (acc.)

§ 12. English will permit some object-verb combinations, as "to babysit, to windowshop, to househunt", but we cannot normally create such phrases as "to waterdrink". However, this is the existing and normal situation in Mongolian and Altaic languages.

§ 15. The archaic ablative, *-dača/-deče*, may also be met, e.g. UD 107a30, *beri-dečegen* (reflexive).

§ 20. Mongolian, instead of much use of personal possessives as *my* and *your*, will employ the reflexive form on that noun possessed.

§ 21—a. An example showing *yeke* 'large, great', normally an adjective, used as a noun, is this.

> PT 3 (71³) *idege umdaya yeke-i* She gave him a large quantity of
> *ögčü* food and drink.

§ 23. The first example, *ayula oi-dur odbai*, could theoretically also mean "the mountain went to the woods" (with two different nouns, this would be more logical), except that no one would obviously read it that way at any time.

§ 24—a. The ending *-nar/-ner* is only for animate creatures.
In general, one may say that in Mongolian the use of a plural form stresses the individual nature of the objects or subjects, rather than the class or category, i.e., not "the students, the books," but "the various students," or "the different books."
Page 22. Under Selection II, in the first line, the sign ‖ means that a new page (folio) began in the original script; it is an aid for anyone who tries to discover the passage in the original document.

§ 29. Gerunds.
29—a. The *-n* converb (gerund of absolute subordination) is frequently well translated by an adverb in English, as "he said in a—manner, as he—ingly said."
Mongolian grammars and reference works have traditionally used a Latin terminology for certain grammatical forms. As it will be helpful for the student to know these terms, they are given here and in the next sections.

gerund of absolute sub-ordination	*-n*	converbum modale
subordinate gerund	*-ču/-ǰu*	converbum imperfecti
coordinative gerund	*-yad*	converbum perfecti

§ 30. infinitive	*-qu/-kü*	nomen futuri
present participle	*-yči*	nomen actoris
preterite participle	*-ysan*	nomen perfecti

29—b. It will help you out of many translation difficulties to know that *-ču/-ǰu* cannot modify a noun, i.e., *ireǰü kümün* "the coming man" is not permissible. Instead, it can modify a verbal noun, e.g., *irejü baiya kümün* "the man who is coming," or *qariju iregsen kümün* "the man who had returned."

§ 31—e. Instrumental. The Latin name is *converbum abtemporale*. In the modern language it frequently has a continuative nuance, and sometimes that meaning will suit a classical text too.

§ 32. Style. As a general hint for translation procedure, it can be stated that the student should find a converb (gerund) terminating a clause (making certain, however, that the converb is not modifying something else), and translate to that point. Then seek the next juncture and translate to there. Never carry a phrase occurring after a converb back to the sense of the preceding clause.

§ 33—b. The example last on the page struck several reviewers as illogical, since the translation (I came, I saw, I conquered) implied a first-person usage. What the Mongolian means, strictly speaking, however is merely "after coming, and after seeing, there was a conquering."

§ 33—c. The verb in -*yu* is sometimes called a gnomic form, or known as the deductive present.

§ 34.

gerund of reporting	-*run*	converbum praeparativum
gerund of purpose	-*ra*	converbum finale
conditional gerund	-*basu*	converbum conditionale
terminative gerund	-*tala*	converbum terminale

The conditional gerund may conveniently be translated by IF when the main verb is future; and by WHEN when the main verb is past. Note especially that -*basu ber* is adversative, i.e., "although."

Page 30, Selection IV, line 11.
The word *bolyan* (today it has a meaning of "each, every," postposed) is "making, as, in the capacity of." The phrase *amitan bolyan sanaju* means "he thought, making into a being" or just "he imagined (a being in the water who had assumed such a shape . . .).

§ 35. The personal pronominal forms are much less used than in Western languages; as noted above, Mongolian is very inclined to use a reflexive possessive in such cases.
Pronouns may also occur immediately after the verb, e.g., *sonusuluya bi* "I have heard"; there is no particular nuance to this.

§ 36. An example of *öber-iyen* used as a subject is the following.
    SK 8a3   *urida öber-iyen yarču*   first he himself came out . . .
                iregsen-dür

§ 37. There are one or two other emphatic forms patterned on *edeger, tedeger,* namely *qotalayar* and *bügüdeger* "they all, all of them."

Whereas English and to a lesser degree, Western European languages, require a pronominal object to finish the sense of a statement, Mongolian is very inclined to leave this unexpressed by any word, though the pronoun is implied in the phrase and may legitimately be added as part of the translation.

UD 21a11 *öggün soyorγa*   Please give (it to me)!

SK 5b9 *bayan-u köbegün-lüge* ... bringing (her) along with
        qamtu abču ireged ...   the rich man's son ...

§ 39. iterative noun   *-daγ*   nomen usus
      continuative noun   *-γa*   nomen imperfecti

§ 40. adversative gerund   *-bač̆u*   converbum concessivum
The same meaning may also be expressed with *-basu ber*.

§ 42. In the last line, read "After *b*, *d*, *g*, *r* and *s* of the stem, the ending is *-ta-/-te-*."

Page 35 (Selection V), footnote 7, better as "when he had grown somewhat".

§ 43. An example of a stem which opposes meanings of these two suffixes is

orulča-   to participate, go in together on
oruldu-   to endeavor, to try

§ 45. Postpositions. English has only a few postposed phrases, such as "the wide world around," or "the door of darkness through" (cf. German *meiner Meinung nach*), but this is the prevailing situation in Mongolian and Altaic languages.

§ 46. Numerals. All of the powers of ten have a separate name in Mongolian, viz.,

arban   ten, 10^1
ǰaγun   hundred, 10^2
mingγan   thousand, 10^3
tümen   ten thousand, myriad, 10^4
bum   hundred thousand, 10^5
saya   million, 10^6
ǰiua   ten million, 10^7
dungšiγur   hundred million, 10^8

There are even higher numbers recorded sporadically, but their meanings become confused, and the sources do not agree with each other.

§ 48. The text (SK 4a1) actually reads *kürügülüged*, but we emended to *kürüged*.

§ 54. Compound Verbs.
The antonym of *čida-* "to be able" is *yada-* "to be unable."
The use of *ab-* as an auxiliary means "to do something suddenly."

SS 66,2   *čuγlaǰu abun*   suddenly assembled

Kh.Gr. 141,6   *ta edüge namayi bayu-*   you get me down from here

                 lγayad ab   right away!

The use of *orki-* "to throw, cast" gives a completive or perfective nuance to the preceding verb. This usage grows more common as we approach modern times. It has become a standard feature of contemporary Buriat, where it renders the Slavic perfective aspect.

A compound with *üje-* "to see" gives a meaning of "to see if one can, to try, to attempt."

     Urga 3,29   *amsaǰu üjesügei*   let me try and taste it

     SK 6b8   *toγolaǰu üjeged*   when he tried to calculate it

There are also a few pronominal verbs in Mongolian, as the stems *yaγa-* "to do what," and *kerki-* "to do how." They are used in Mongolian where English or a Western language would use an interrogative "why" or "how."

§ 58 (New Section). Subtle Shift of Subject

Mongolian is not obligated to express a subject with every verb. Generally speaking, of course, it is self-evident from the context and general sense of the narrative, but very often a clause or sentence is grammatically impersonal, i.e., "there was a going," or "there was a being," though we know that to translate "he went," or "they were" is the only sensible thing to do. To be aware of this will aid you many times in translating.

As a result of this, it sometimes happens that the subject at the end of a sentence may not be the same as at the beginning—in the middle there has been what I term a "subtle shift of subject." The sense always makes it clear who is doing what, but unless you are prepared for such a shift, you will be confused. The following is a good example.

     SK 4b2—3   *tere qaγan ber ... oduγad*   The Khan ... proceeded, and

               kejiye sidintü kegür-i üjeged   when he beheld the Bewitched

               üldegsen-dür, amiri neretü   Corpse, gave chase, and he

               modun-dur abiraǰu odbai.   [not the Khan, but the Bewitched Corpse!] went and climbed the mango tree.

In modern grammatical terms, one might say that the surface structure has no subject, but the deep structure has a subject.

Page 49 (Selection VI), part 3, lines 18—19.

This is poetry, and should be divided this way:

     nigültü kilinča üiledbesü,
     amitan tamu-dur unayu;
     buyan üiledbesü,
     degedü sain töröl-dür töröyü.

Supplement to the Glossary

Note that these entries are in an ordinary A to Z order. Some entries are new listings; others correct or give new meanings to existing entries; some apply to the supplemental readings book.

ab ali whatever
abči- to bring, fetch.
abiri- to mount, climb up
abulča- to promise
abun alda- to almost catch
ači tusa good deed
alban üje- to pay taxes
aman abu- to promise
amsa- to taste
amurliyuluyči = amurčiyuluyči
aryada- to employ means, persuade
atala as long as, while

ba bürün = ba bürin all of us; universal
bari- 1. to take, seize, catch
        2. to build, erect, construct
        3. to present an offering
-basu ber although
Bede proper name (old name of Mongols)
beriye club, cudgel
beye bildar body and appearance
bol-: ese bol- to disagree
  boluyujai I wonder if it would be possible
busu: preposed: other, different
        postposed: not, without
bütü- to produce, fabricate

čing firm, firmly

daila- to cope, compete
  dailalda- to be hospitable, to entertain
darbayulya streamer
degere upon
dil = del mane
doytunalabai = dotunalabai showed favoritism
doloyoyana red berry
doroidayul- to lay low, humble
düri intention
dvib continent

ed see *tavar*
-eče busu apart from, except
egerijü = erijü seeking
elige uruyu stomach-down
ese bol- to disagree

yadanaši out in front
yociqa (Manchu *gōcika*) subject, adjutant, subordinate
yodoli ball-pointed arrow (to stun birds)

geigsen the one who shed illumination
gele it has been said
gengsigür-tele to the point of lamenting, wailing, bemoaning

in = yin genitive

jabdu- to be about to, to almost
jergeber simultaneous
jiyala- read *jiyalya-* to teach

kabalik city name, distorted form of Cambaluc, or of Kapalivastu
kenggerge drum
ker ki- to do how (also *kerki-*)
kerem a kind of fish
keüken also: girl
kötel-, kötöl- correct to:
  ködel- to move
  kötül- to lead, conduct

mede- to learn, find out, know; also, to rule, dispose
musaragi opal (or another precious stone)

Nāgārjuna proper name, Buddhist saint
namaji for *namayi* me
namur fall (season)
nasun-a tegüldür 'perfect in life', a disciple
nima form of **i* he

olanta many times
onila- to nock (set arrow to bow)
oroi 1. top 2. late
  naran oroi bol- night falls
oros Russian, European

öči- to say (from lower to higher);
  to address, intone, depose; to
  speak respectfully to
ögedele- to go upstream
ögüle- same as *ügüle-* to speak
ögte- to be given
öni for a long time

pad (Skt. phaṭ) a mystical syllable

qaγarqai split, broken
qairala- to bestow
qalun read *γal-un* "of fire"
qataγuji- to endure hardship
qadum betrothed
qoitu future (not "past")
qudal deceit, false, counterfeit

sakiγulsun totem, *genius*
soqur blind

šibtura- to slip down
šimgü- to nestle, snuggle
šiqa- to peer·

tail- to take off (boots)
terigüten "etc., the other things"

tedüi size, so much as
tiib see *dvip*
toγosun dust
tokiya- to coincide, occur together
  (not *dokiya-*)
tosu- to receive, get, accept
tul- to support
tuqai on account of, because of

uγuγata completely
uiradučila- (*oγiradučila-*) read
  uridučila- to do as before
unin = *utaγan* smoke, mist
  unin-u morin smoke horse (i.e.,
  a horse made of the smoke)
urala- to be a craftsman
urid former
  uridaki that in the previous
urtuγulin length
uruγ relatives
urus- to drift, float

üge-ber bol- to comply, agree
ügei after two nouns = "and"
ülü bol- to be impossible, not be
  permitted
ündüsün root, foundation, basis

viγagirid (Skt. *vyakṛta*) prophecy

yaγu ba nothing at all
yambar bu whatever, any kinf of
yosuγar according to